TEARS OF A CLOWN

VOLUME 1

Dr. George B. Jackson

Copyright © 2013 Dr. George B. Jackson

Revision August 29, 2013, 2nd Publication

All rights reserved. No part of this book may be reproduced in any form or by any means without prior consent of the author, except in brief quotes used in reviews. To request more information in this matter send a request to cfcf01@triad.twcbc.com.

Scriptures taken from the Holy Bible, King James Version
© 2011-2013 unless otherwise noted.

Editor & Book Cover Design – Pamela S. Jackson

Pureheart Publishing, Thomasville, NC 27360

ISBN: 148487448X
ISBN: 13: 978-1484874486

Memoirs of a Gospel Preacher

For after that in the wisdom of God the world by wisdom knew not God, it pleased God by the foolishness of preaching to save them that believe (1 Corinthians 1:21).

Dedication

To my lovely wife Pamela, for your unconditional love and support of all my dreams and visions; to my children: Marquis Catrell, Antoine Gregory, Monica Nicole, Ashton Jamel, Phillip Michael and Martin George…the fullness of my quiver,
the good people of all the churches I have planted:
New Covenant Missionary Baptist Church,
Rock Hill, SC;
Citadel of Faith Christian Fellowship,
Thomasville, NC;
Citadel of Hope Christian Fellowship, Lancaster, SC;
Citadel of Joy Christian Fellowship, Greensboro, NC
and the administration and staff of
United Cornerstone School of Divinity,
Thomasville, NC.

KNOWLEDGE IS NEVER WISDOM UNTIL IT IS SHARED...
~ DR. GEORGE B. JACKSON

TABLE OF CONTENTS

INTRODUCTION	1
CHAPTER 1	
ENCOURAGEMENT	
God of the Recession	6
The Necessity of Preaching	11
The Thud of Silence	15
God Has Not Forgotten	18
But I Thought it Was a Weed	21
Fret Not Thyself	24
A Resurrection Revelation	31
CHAPTER 2	
FAITH	
Your Labor is Not in Vain	42
After the Rain	45
There's No Place Like Home	50
The Urgency of Now	61
Ten Reasons To Be Thankful	69
Lost and Found	79
I Feel Like Bustin Loose	82
CHAPTER 3	
PRAISE	
The Theory of Praise	98
The King of the Jungle	102
Fight the Power	105
From Tragedy to Triumph	110
It's Electric	118
Another Night With the Frogs	132
I Can't Hold My Peace	146
The Expedient Route	156

INTRODUCTION

Why the Tears of a Clown?

While Christianity is not inherent, as is Judaism or nationalistic like Islam, it seems that my Christian pilgrimage began before my birth. My father, Dr. William T. Jackson, Sr. continued a succession of preachers by accepting the call to preach in 1952, at the age of 22. I was born in 1962 while he pastored Weeping Mary Baptist Church in Boiling Green, South Carolina.

Growing up I never wanted to preach. I loved the drama and intensity of worship in the church, but I fought conformity. When you are raised in the house of a pastor you see and hear things that make you bitter. My mother was very passive and my dad was often intimidated by the congregations he served. I remember one very unpleasant church meeting during my teen years when my mother was so offended and my dad was being fussed out by church members. That was enough to make me weary of the church and I vowed never to preach.

I began studying Islam in college, but found it unfulfilling. Drifting further from the church, I ended up working at the Gaston Boys Club in Gastonia, North Carolina after finishing North Carolina Central University in Durham. The stress from dealing with sometimes unmanageable boys, ages 6 to 18 years old and their parents caused me to pray again. I began to ease my way back into church. A year later (1986), I was actively involved in a local church.

One night in November of that year, I was reciting Dr. King's, "*I Have a Dream*" speech at a community function. In the midst of delivery, the Lord spoke to my heart. His voice said, "You will do greater things than this if you follow me". When I finished the speech, I rushed home and fell on my face before the Lord.

Late that night in tears, I called home and announced to my parents, "I've been called to preach". I preached my first sermon (at 24 years old) at the church my dad served for 33 years. I was licensed in December 1986, ordained in 1987 and began my first pastorate in October 1988. This Christian journey has taken me through the vicissitudes of life. The Lord has led me to pastor and plant churches in both Carolinas and Philadelphia, Pennsylvania.

INTRODUCTION

Twenty-six years later I realize that my pilgrimage was impacted by many years growing up in church parsonages. I started writing articles and short stories in 2001 during the midst of a crisis. Unlike lengthy sermons which require interpretation, exposition and exegesis, the articles came easy and were often shaped by life experiences and current events. This is a collection of writings over a 12 year slice of my life and ministry that reflects my views, opinions and theology. Some pieces were written in triumph and some in tragedy. Some were written in great joy, others in a tide of tears. Through it all I have come to understand what the Apostle Paul meant when he told the Corinthian Church, "for since in the Wisdom of God the world through its wisdom did not know Him, God was pleased through the *foolishness* of what was preached to save those who believe" (1 Cor. 1:21).

My greatest joy and most strenuous labor has been in the planting of churches. Along the way, God has blessed me to baptize and lead many people to Christ. While this road has been rough at times, I must admit, "Nobody told me that the road would be easy, I don't believe He brought me this far, to leave me".

CHAPTER 1

ENCOURAGEMENT

God of the Recession	6
The Necessity of Preaching	11
The Thud of Silence	15
God Has Not Forgotten	18
But I Thought It Was a Weed	21
Fret Not Thyself	24
A Resurrection Revelation	31

GOD OF THE RECESSION

Before the mountains were brought forth, or ever thou hadst formed the earth and the world, even from everlasting to everlasting, thou art God (Psalm 90:2).

Perhaps only Isaiah 40 can compare with this Psalm of Moses written around 1500 BC in presenting God's grandeur and eternity in contrast to our frailty and mortality. Moses' point, however, is that God's eternity is the answer to our problems with time and the precarious situations it puts us in.

Currently we find ourselves in the midst of one of the most severe financial crisis we have seen in half a century. Some analysts call it a Bear Market. We know it better as a Recession.

Recession is when the state of the economy declines; a widespread decline in the Gross Domestic Product and high unemployment, lasting from six months to two years. Recession affects people economically, mentally, physically and even spiritually.

So how did we arrive at this most unpleasant point of transition? What were some of the factors leading to the current worldwide recession? Who shall we blame?

The housing bubble burst. Investors reaped diminishing returns. There was blatant greed, ambition and vanity in the financial sector. Factories experienced massive layoffs. There was little to no federal oversight of the stock market. The banking industry was crippled by corruption and excessiveness. The current unemployment figures are at a 30 year high; streets were littered with foreclosure signs. Bankruptcy filings in 2008 were up 31 percent over 2007 figures, while dozens of investment companies collapsed.

Recession is not a new economic trend unique only to modern western civilization. Famines (a form of natural recession) are recorded in the time of Abraham (Genesis 12:10; 2:10) "And there was a famine in the land: and Abram went down into Egypt to sojourn there; for the famine [was] grievous in the land,") of Isaac (Genesis 26:1), "And there was a famine in the land, beside the first famine that was in the days of Abraham. And Isaac went unto Abimelech king of the Philistines unto Gerar," of Jacob, when Joseph was in Egypt – seven years of famine even after seven of plenty (Genesis 41:54), "And the seven years of dearth began to come, according as Joseph had said: and the dearth was in all lands; but in all the land of Egypt there was bread,") and, indeed, "was over all the face of the earth" (Genesis 41:56, "And the famine was over all the face of the earth: And Joseph opened all the storehouses, and sold unto the Egyptians; and the famine waxed sore in the land of Egypt").

The story of the prodigal son told by Jesus in the form of a parable is about an ungrateful people and their personal excessiveness which led to indiscriminate wastefulness; about how a flamboyant and lavish lifestyle can lead to a decline; about how abject poverty and self-examination can lead to recovery.

In our individual and collective recessions, we must somehow retain hope. God's people cannot let this recession lead to depression and ultimately concession to the desires of the enemy who wants to see us give up and concede defeat.

Recession or the bear market is a normal part of the economic cycle. Dry seasons are a part of the natural cycle of life. Trial and tribulation are tests we must pass in order to trigger our testimony. If we don't go through some hell in this life, we won't appreciate the glory yet to come. Paul declared in Romans 8:18, "For I reckon that the sufferings of this present time (are) not worthy (to be compared) with the glory which shall be revealed in us."

In the last 110 years, there has been 24 declared recessions, but the nation has recovered from them all.[1] Recession is usually preceded by a period of widespread prosperity. The events of September 11, 2001, created a worldwide panic and closed global stock markets only to be followed by an unprecedented explosion in the housing market. No matter the calamity we have faced as a nation, God has brought us through it all! No wonder Edward Mote declared, "My hope is built on nothing less than Jesus' blood and righteousness."[2]

It might be hidden to us now the outcome of this international turmoil, but I'm going to trust God anyway. I'm going on faith and not on sight. "Jesus saith unto him, Thomas, because thou hast seen me, thou hast believed: blessed [are] they that have not seen, and [yet] have believed" (John 20:29).

---

[1] U.S. Business Cycle Expansions and Contractions, *Nation Bureau of Economic Research*, 2009
[2] Mote, Edward, "*Hymns of Praise*", 1836

He is the God of the Recession because he contends with what we contend with. He is the God of the Recession because He's the same yesterday, today and forever. I would encourage you to stand still a little longer and see the salvation of the Lord.

We are going to emerge from this recession victorious because Jesus shed blood is the stimulus that already bailed us out! One Friday evening he died for a sin cursed world, but early on Sunday morning he got up from the dead with all power (including economic power) in His hands.

~ August 1, 2009

The Necessity of Preaching

In the biblical classic of Jonah in the belly of the great fish, we see an obscure Galilean prophet attempting to run from God. The prophet went to a port city named Joppa to purchase a ticket on the fleetest ship sailing for Tarshish a city of southern Spain. In that day Tarshish, was the farthest point to which sea fairing vessels could travel . Like Jacob, (in Genesis 28) Jonah thought that God was territorial, confined to Israel. Jonah soon found out that the God of Israel was indeed universal. He even controls the elements of nature. The great fish that swallowed the castaway prophet validated this truth. God is inescapable.

Many people have called Jonah hardheaded or stubborn. While this statement bears some truth, it fails to shed light on the complexities of Jonah's situation. He was a preacher who did not want to go to unexplored territory to start a new church. He was comfortable where he was and complacency caused him to run, in fear, from the command of God.

One of the major themes of the Holy Bible is preaching. There are 137 references to or about preaching in the scriptures, dating back to Nehemiah in 426 BC, Jesus the Christ in the Gospels and concluding with the Revelation of Saint John in 100 AD.

Preaching has long been controversial, a virtual hot bed for contention. Solomon, the third King of Israel, called himself Ecclesiastes; or the preacher, declaring; "Vanity of vanities,. . . all is vanity" (Ecclesiastes 12:8). The message of the preacher is not always popular or received with open arms. Because of his preaching, Jeremiah of Anathoth was cast into prison by Pashur. When Ezekiel (during Israel's captivity in Babylon) preached, Pelatiah the son of Benaiah fell dead. Belshazzar, king of the Chaldeans was murdered the same night that Daniel proclaimed that the handwriting was on the wall. Amos the shepherd preacher from Tekoa was threatened with death and kicked out of the royal sanctuary at Bethel for his uncompromising preaching. Ten of the 12 disciples of Jesus Christ were martyred for preaching the gospel.

Yet with all the adversity that the art has faced, preaching is still essential for salvation. Paul wrote to the church at Corinth; "For after that in the wisdom of God the world by wisdom knew not God, it pleased God by the foolishness of preaching to save them that believe," (Corint.1:21).

The preacher must be cognizant of the fact that everything is on the line when he stands behind the holy desk to preach Christ and Him crucified, dead, buried, and resurrected on the third day morning. The church cannot expect to draw lost men to Jesus without powerful, dynamic, soul stirring preaching. Edward T. Hiscox said, "The true object and design of preaching is to bring people to Christ and to help them grow in their Christian discipleship. Instruction may properly be said to be the first object of preaching. Most emphatically it is not to entertain an audience, not to crowd the house with hearers, nor to build up wealthy and fashionable congregations, nor to replenish the treasury, nor to teach literature, science, or art but to save and nurture souls by an exhibition of Christ crucified. For this purpose our Lord designated 'some pastors and teachers, for the perfecting of the saints, for the work of the ministry, for the edifying of the body of Christ' (Eph. 4:11, 12)."[3]

---

[3] Hiscox, Edward T., *Hiscox Guide for Baptist Churches*, pg. 1964

While the pastor of a church has a multiplicity of responsibilities ranging from the executive to the custodial, there is nothing more important than in-depth, effective, well-planned, goal-oriented, Holy Ghost anointed preaching. Church members need constant motivation. They receive such when their fearless leader stands up to preach. My father, Dr. William T. Jackson, has told me on several occasions, "Son, never be found guilty of not preaching."

~June 18, 2003

The Thud of Silence

"Then everyone deserted him and fled" ~ *(Mark 14:50)*

The prelude to Mark 14:50 is the emphatic declaration of loyalty and solidarity intimated by Peter and the disciples. After sharing the Passover meal Jesus and his beloved friends walked over to the Mount of Olives. There he challenged their resolve to follow Him. He told them that they would soon abandon Him and run away.

Peter and the other disciples insisted that they would never leave Jesus. A few hours later as He was about to depart from the Garden of Gethsemane, a mob led by Judas Iscariot apprehended Jesus. Ironically, the same group that declared their undying allegiance to the Master a few hours earlier scattered like chickens into the night. All that was left was the thud of silence.

Since the massacre of six faculty and 20 children at Newtown, Connecticut on December 14, 2012, I have watched many silent prayer vigils and public memorials for the innocent victims. I've heard the declarations of solidarity with the victims' families and the Sandy Hook School community. Politicians made many promises to help them get through this horrific tragedy and then the thud of silence. Silence on the ban of the sale and manufacture of automatic and semi-automatic weapons of war and mass destruction. Silence on high capacity ammunition clips. Silence on illegal gun trafficking. Even silence on universal background checks for legal gun sales. Maybe we have become numb or desensitized to gun violence in our nation. Homicide, suicide, mass murder it's an everyday thing in America. Why should we be alarmed? Why question or challenge what has become the status-quo? American poet, Ella Wheeler Wilcox said, *"To sin by silence when they should protest makes cowards of men."*[4]

As an ordained clergy I am ashamed of myself for not speaking out about this national epidemic that impacts too many people I know and love. Of all the mission work we do, the protection and care of the children (whom our Savior loved and made special provision for) should be paramount. How many massacres are enough to make the houses of worship in our country break the code of silence and demand gun law reform?

---

[4] Wilcox, Ella Wheeler, *Poems of Problems*, 1914 pg. 154

Holocaust survivor and 1986 Nobel Prize Winner Elie Wiesel declared, *"I swore never to be silent whenever and wherever human beings endure suffering and humiliation. We must take sides. Neutrality helps the oppressor, never the victims. Silence encourages the tormentor never the tormented."*[5]

There must be more we can do to speak to the conscious of America. Two thousand years ago Jesus Christ was abandoned by those who should have demanded his acquittal and protested his conviction. Forty-five years ago on April 4, 1968, Dr. Martin Luther King Jr. was shot down by a high-powered rifle because he would not be quiet about the infirmities of the nation he so loved. Dr. King said, *"History will have to record that the greatest tragedy of this period of social transition was not the strident clamor of the bad people, but the appalling silence of the good people."*[6]

~ March 26, 2013

---

[5] Wiesel, Elie, *Nobel Prize Acceptance Speech*, 1986
[6] King, Martin Luther Jr., *Remaining Awake Through a Great Revolution*, Oberlin College, 1965

God Has Not Forgotten

"How long wilt thou forget me. O Lord? Forever? How long wilt thou hide thy face from me? (Psalms 13:1)

A millennium before the advent of Jesus the Christ the prophet Samuel anointed Jesse's youngest son, David, king of Israel. There was only one problem, Saul was already king. David was in a precarious position. He was living in the royal palace, an officer in the king's army. He married the king's daughter, Michal and was best friend to the king's son Jonathan. The people loved David, memorializing him, in song. The insecure Saul became jealous and plotted to kill young David. Abandoning all of his earthly comforts and luxuries, David fled from Saul. Being hunted and trapped like a wild animal David was helpless. He feels hopeless and removed from God. In the throes of despair David laments, "How long wilt thou forget me, O Lord?

Three thousand years later, that same sentiment prevails. People still wonder about God's concern during man's dilemmas. Did God forget to protect us from the unprecedented carnage of September 11, 2001? What about the almost four years of drought that has devastated our region? Did the AIDS virus just slip by him unnoticed? Is the crisis in the Middle East some typographical error on the Lord's behalf?

We've all prayed earnestly for the Lord to do something on our behalf only to be met with silence. We've waited on God to move and nothing appeared to happen. I know God is omniscient, but it seems that He is often too busy to address my situation when I want Him to.

Where was God when mother was to her deathbed? Where was He when father died with cancer? Where was He when my job shut down . . . my mortgage was past due . . . my husband left me . . . my wife rejected me? During the storms of life we wonder . . . Has God forgotten about me?

Here's good news . . . You are important to God! You are His most cherished creation. God loves us so much that He made us in His own image, after His own likeness. This same David that felt so abandoned in Psalms 13 would later sing in Psalms 139, "I will praise thee, for I am fearfully and wonderfully made."

This God never sleeps nor slumbers. His eye searches the entire universe. He has even numbered the very hairs upon your head. He thinks of you so much that He turned love into propitiation (sacrifice) and surrendered His only begotten Son, the Lord Jesus the Christ, to die on Calvary on your personal behalf. No, God has not forgotten. He is watching. He is moving on your behalf. Every tick of the clock is a reminder that God continues to hold the world in His hand.

Maybe the real problem is we have forgotten God. We've taken Him for granted. We do not talk to Him until we are about to fall asleep at night. We often overlook Him in times of prosperity, vitality, and peace. We leave Him at home when we go to school or the ball game or social events.

It often takes a failure, dilemma, or tragedy to remind us that He is just a prayer away. He's waiting with open arms to hold you during your turmoil. He has a unique plan developed to deliver you from whatever you are going through and contend with what you contend with; but right now it is so hard to understand. That is because His thoughts are not our thoughts and His ways are not our ways. ~ August, 2005

But I Thought It Was A Weed

Early one fall morning my mother woke me up to go out and cut the grass. I was home from college on fall break and cutting grass was the last thing on my mind. Still half asleep, I stumbled out to the backyard to crank up the lawnmower. I figured I could run the mower across the yard and return to bed.

In my dazed haste I ran over what looked like several large, wild blades of grass. My mother walked out the door in time to see her young flowers cut to shreds. She screamed at the top of her voice to get my attention ... "Hey you big dummy, you just cut down my flowers." I looked around at the plants on the lawn. I cut off the mower and said in my most sincere pitiful voice, I'm sorry mom, but I thought it was a weed!

Sometimes in our anxiousness and self – righteousness we try to do God's job and pull up weeds. It's hard to tell wheat from tares, especially when the two are young because wheat looks like grass, it is bright green in color. Too often we want to cut down something without seeing if it bears fruit ... The only way you can know a tree is by the fruit it bears. And trees don't bear fruit overnight. It takes time for fruit to develop and ripen.

We try to do God's job and say who's called or not called. We want to determine who's sincere and who's fake. Who reaches our standards and fails to measure up to us. We want everybody to pass our personal litmus test as if we cast the deciding ballot on heaven or hell.

Regardless of the expertise of the farmer there are going to be weeds in the field. Every church shall have problems, whether it's in the usher ministry, choir, missionary circle, pew or pulpit. The devil is going to sow weeds everywhere, that's his job. David warns us not to fret because of evil doers, neither be envious against the workers of iniquity.

Eventually, the green blade shall mature a golden brown. Then the Lord of Host shall separate the wheat from the tares, the just from the unjust, the right from the wrong. God shall cast the enemy into eternal fire. There will be great weeping and gnashing of teeth. But the righteous shall sit at the welcome table in glory with the Lord.

Jesus said in the parable of the wheat and the tares "Let both grow together until the harvest: and in the time of harvest I will say to the reapers gather ye together first the tares and bind them in bundles to burn them but gather the wheat into my barn (Matt 13:30)." In other words let God be God. Let God be the gardener. The last word belongs to him, for he is too prudent to make a mistake; too sovereign to do wrong. Beware of hasty judgments. A poet once wrote, "When you get to heaven you will likely view many folk there who'll be a shock to you. But don't act surprised or even show a care, for they might be a little shocked to see you standing there."

~ September 24, 2003

Fret Not Thyself
Psalm 37: 1-3

TEXT – *¹ Fret not thyself because of evil doers, neither be thou envious against the workers of iniquity. ² For they shall be cut down like the grass and wither as the green herb. ³Trust in the Lord, and do good; so shalt thou dwell in the land, and verily thou shalt be fed.*

EXPOSITION - Unlike other Psalms or songs of praise, the Jewish Maschil is a lament or sermon of wisdom and instruction which encourages us to ponder over or understand. This sermon of sorts was written approximately 1000 BC. King David, the sweet psalmist of Israel, was often disturbed by the prosperity, abundance and the palatal luxury enjoyed by evil doers.

INTRODUCTION - Why do those who are evil prosper? Where was God's wrath? When will justice prevail? In the Old Testament, God promised believers like Abraham, Job and Solomon earthly and material prosperity. Our hope today is not in earthen vessels but in heaven. David instructs us not to fret or worry about the underserved gains of the corrupt, for God will have judgment on them.

DEF - Fret (Hebrew – "charah") to be angry, burn; Webster describes "fret" as a verb meaning displeased, to irritate, vex, worry, fume, complain or eat away at.

I. Often we find ourselves fretting about evildoers (Hebrew – "raw-ah", bad good for naught, wicked, baser sort).
   1. The wicked seem to advance while the obedient suffer. . .
      a. The self-indulgent and self-righteous flourish and prosper.
      b. The children of God struggle to make ends meet .
      c. The greedy want more; the rich get richer at the expense of the proletariat.
      d. The humble and meek endure hard trials daily. . . Yes, evil seems to dominate the globe.
      e. Reports of crime, corruption, drug abuse and wars are the headlines of the day.
      f. Evils' temporal success becomes alluring , attractive even magnetic to those who a easily deceived.

2. Many a good man has turned to evil's convenience, the temptation of the quick fix; the attractiveness and accessibility of the pleasure principle. The concept that if it feels good you ought to "do it till you're satisfied".
3. In a dog eat dog world it seems useless to continue to do good, there seems to be no profit or advantage in righteous living. Nice guys seem to always finish last.
4. I guess Paul was right . . . "When I would do good, evil is present with me (Rom 7:21)."

II. Asaph was envious of the prosperity of the evil until he entered the sanctuary of God and realized that one day the wicked would be cut down like the grass and wither like weeds. This explains Jesus telling the disciples at Jerusalem to "Strive to enter in at the strait gate! (Matthew 13:24) He told them to raise a standard, not compromise the faith. "Lift your heads for your redemption draweth nigh (Luke 21:28)."

1. Evil shall not see the kingdom of God. The ungodly are like the dust which the wind blows away ... They shall be... denied a seat in the kingdom.
2. But the righteous . . . "He shall be like a tree planted by the rivers of waters . . . his leaf shall not wither; and whatsoever he doeth shall prosper". When the evil ones seem to

advance and prosper, don't be discouraged, disenchanted, disheartened or dismayed. As Jesus told the church in Smyrna, "Fear none of those things which thou shalt suffer: behold, the devil shall cast some of you into prison, that ye may be tried; and ye shall have tribulation 10 days: be thou faithful unto death, and I will give thee a crown of life" (Rev 2:10).

III. Your time on this planet is too precious to be envious against the workers of iniquity.
   1. Often we are envious of the wealth of the wicked; we want to trade places with them, indulge in their glory and lifestyles.
   2. Our petty jealousy, our envy is our own punishment because it causes an uneasiness of the spirit, it robs us of our joy, it stymies our motivation and gives Satan leverage against us.
   3. Our envy spreads like a virus in our lives. We start to envy everyone about everything. Nothing makes us happy. We complain and gripe about anything; nick-picking and nagging about the least little thing.

4. Can't you see fretting will make you lose weight . . . lose hair . . . lose sleep . . . lose your sanity . . . lose your faith and miss your blessings.

IV. At the appointed time God shall cut evil down like a blade of grass. Evil will blow away like the sand on the seashore.
1. The end of evil has already been declared. Jesus promised that one day . . . "there shall be no more curse; but the throne of God and of the lamb shall be in it; and his servants shall serve him" (Rev 2:3).
2. The same David who sympathized with our worries understood that "Many are the afflictions of the righteous but the Lord delivereth him out of them all" (Psa 34:19).
3. Evil is transitory, negative, can't last, finite. It will wither like the green herb. I believe that no lie can live forever; truth crushed to the earth shall rise again. 19th Century poet James Russell Lowell once said, "Truth forever on the scaffold, wrong forever on the throne. Yet, that scaffold sways the future, for behind that scaffold in the dim unknown stands God, keeping watch over his own".

One day the wicked shall be tuned into hell.[7] The enemies of God shall be humbled. For unto him every knee shall bow and every tongue confess that He is Lord (Phil 2:10).

TRANSITION - Adolf Hitler was the powerful, evil leader of Nazi Germany. His blitzkrieg trampled over Poland, Czechoslovakia, Austria and France. He was supposed to be indestructible . . . But God cut him down. God toppled his government; for there is no place in His holy providence for the permanence of evil. I know it gets rough sometimes, but hold on! I know you're mistreated and abused for no apparent reason but remain steadfast.

CONCLUSION - Weeping may endure for a night, but joy is soon to come in the morning light. God will wipe all tears from your eyes, all problems from your family, all hell hounds and evil enemies from our trail. I know the devil is trying to kill you but remember, "No weapon formed against thee shall prosper: and every tongue that shall rise against thee in judgment, thou shalt condemn. This is the heritage of the servants of the Lord" (Isa 54:17). Wait on

---

[7] Lowell, James Russell, *The Present Crisis*, 1914

the Lord and be of good courage and he shall strengthen thine heart . . . For they that wait upon the Lord shall renew their strength! When evil seems to be winning, I'm still happy because what the enemy meant for evil, the Lord meant it for good to save much people alive! Though your enemy means you no good, be thankful that, "All things work together for good to them that love God, to them who are called according to His purpose" (Rom 8:28). Your day is coming! You're going to be the head and not the tail, the top and not the bottom, the lender and not the borrower. You're going to reap crops you have not planted . . . live in houses you did not build. For the wealth of the sinner is laid up for the just. And we are the righteousness of God.

~July 6, 2003

A Resurrection Revelation
Philippians 3:10 & 11

TEXT – *That I may know him and the power of his resurrection, and the fellowship of his suffering, being made conformable unto his death; If by any means I might attain unto the resurrection of the dead (NIV).*

EXPOSITION - Paul's letter to the Philippian church is one of several prison letters. It was not drafted from Nero's Mamertine dungeon as in his farewell letter in II Timothy; but from his rented abode, where he was under house arrest in AD 61, in the capital city of Rome. This magnificent treatise was the apostle's vehicle to thank the Philippian church for the love offering they sent him in detention. In that Philippi was a prosperous Roman colony in Macedonia, the church was able to gather enough funds to help their founding pastor pay for his room and board in Rome.

It seems that Philippi was an important city in the gold-producing region east of Rome. It was originally named for Phillip II, the father of Alexander the Great. Through it ran a great highway known as the Via Egnatia that led to Rome in the West and Neapolis where Paul landed to answer the Macedonian call in the East. It was in Philippi that Paul went to a Sabbath day prayer meeting on the banks of the Gangites River. It was there that Lydia, a seller of purple, first heard the gospel preached and gave her life to Jesus. Obviously, there were not enough Jews in Philippi to establish a synagogue and so the apostle's language here is conversant to Gentiles or Hellenist.

INTRODUCTION - In this encouraging letter, the Apostle is thankful to God for the congregation of believers. He is not ashamed of his personal hardship, being a prisoner under the eye of an armed guard. Paul believes that his issues have been God's opportunity to advance the gospel of Jesus Christ. The missionary then admonishes the church to be consistent in the gospel. He told them to take courage in the face of opposition. In essence, live a life worthy of the gospel. He told them to stick together having one mind, one love and one spirit. But not only that, Paul wanted this young church to take responsibility for its actions, to take care of the business of winning souls and defending the faith. He prayed that the people would at least try to live holy, blameless and upright. In this they could rejoice even in bad times for they would exemplify the servant attitude of Christ.

EXEGESIS - In chapter three, Paul draws the church close to his bosom to protect her with a warning to beware of "dogs," people who glory in the law or in the rules or in custom or tradition. These Judaizers or legalistic zealots, who demanded that the gentiles be circumcised, were guilty of elevating the law (which got its strength from sin) over faith (which keeps its strength through the knowledge of Jesus Christ). The understanding of these religious thugs was only through the law and, therefore, only through the flesh. There is no righteousness in the flesh (for all righteousness is as a filthy rag). There is no holiness in the flesh; therefore, no hope in the corruptible flesh. The apostle, speaking in the supernatural, desires to "know Him," experience Him and embrace Him, in the beauty of holiness. The only way he can achieve this enlightened state of being is by a "Resurrection Revelation."

I. Paul wanted the congregation to know that this knowledge is not merely factual, historical, or empirical; but, it is also inclusive of the awesome power of our Savior's resurrection.

A RESURRECTION REVELATION

1. It was indeed Jesus who preached an immutable doctrine of resurrection, contrary to the Sadducees, who denied that there was life after death.
2. Jesus explained to grieving Martha of Bethany whose brother Lazarus had been dead four days, "I am the resurrection and the life: he that believeth in me though he were dead, yet shall he live: And whosoever liveth and believeth in me shall never die" (John 11:25 – 26).
3. Therefore, He is Lord of the Resurrection, giving eternal life to the righteous and eternal punishment to the wicked.
4. The apostle rejoiced in resurrection as the final, glorious event, ushering Christians out of the physical conflict of the present age into holistic glory, which will be revealed in the saints when Jesus comes again.
5. In resurrection, God's new creation will embrace final, perpetual completion. That's why John declared, "Beloved, now we are the sons of God, and it doth not yet appear what we shall be; but we know that when he shall appear, we shall be like Him; for we shall see Him as He is" (1 John 3:2).

6. The foundation of hope for Christian's is the resurrection of our Savior from a borrowed grave. Without his resurrection, there would be no gospel or "good news" to preach. No songs about victory to sing. No petitions about another chance to pray. No testimonies about being tried in the fire and coming out like pure gold to share with the saints.

TRANSITION - There would be no need to dance in the aisle or wave holy hands had He not risen on the third day morning with all power in His hands.

II. The apostle asserts that in order to experience divine acquaintance with Jesus, we must be able to comprehend divine suffering.

  1. It is fascinating to us that God would send His only begotten Son into an evil world where He would experience all levels of pain and suffering. The Father, Himself is affected by the sufferings of the Son on the Cross. God is not immune to human agony.

  2. While Jesus' excruciating suffering was unique to Him, without our vicariously entering into His suffering, we will not be able to cope with our own miniscule grieves and pains. We would be

consumed by our tears and sorrows, wallowing in a cesspool of proclivity, groveling in a quagmire of self-pity.

3. The early church recognized the inevitability of suffering. They were always under fire, always under attack from without and within. Yet, somehow they endured. Somehow they remained united.

4. They concluded, "If we suffer, we shall also reign with Him" (II Tim 2:12). If we deny Him, He also will deny us. "And whether one member suffers, all the members rejoice with it" (1 Cor 12:26).

5. If we are serious about carrying out His mandate, we shall endure hard trials and tribulation, because the world hates us as much as it hates our Risen Savior.

6. Stop expecting unbelievers to treat you kindly because you're saved and sanctified now.

7. Stop expecting the enemy to give you a break because you've been born again and washed in the blood of the Lamb.

8. Stop expecting your enemies to be nice to you because you have a diamond-studded, gold cross bling-blinging around your neck.
9. Stop expecting the hellhounds to quit chasing you just because you danced and fell out at church the other Sunday.
10. Stop expecting folks who have never spoke to you, to suddenly start speaking to you because you pay your tithe without being asked.
11. Don't you realize that under the altar in glory are "the souls of them that were slain for the word of God and the testimony which they held" (Rev. 6:9).

TRANSITION - So suffering for His sake is a privilege; a promotion; even a prerequisite to a Resurrection Revelation. His brother James said, "My Brethren, count it all joy when you fall into diver's temptation: Knowing this, that the trying of your faith worketh patience" (James 1:2-3).

   III. Yet to really know Him, you must be bold enough to risk it all and die with Him, even to suffer death on the cross.

1. When Thomas realized that Jesus was determined to return to Bethany to awake Lazarus from eternal sleep even though the Jews sought to kill Him, he said to his fellow disciples, "Let us go that we may die with Him" (John 11:16).
2. It seems that everybody wants to go to heaven and yet nobody wants to die. It's the ultimate offering and the supreme sacrifice. It's an appointment that you can't break no matter how preoccupied you are.
3. Job was curious about death. He asked rhetorically, "If a man die, shall he live again? All the days of my appointed time will I wait 'til my change comes" (Job 14:14).
4. As wise as he was, Job did not know about a wonderful Savior named Jesus. He had no idea that out of Nazareth would rise, "The root and the offspring of David, the bright and morning star" (Rev 22:16).
5. The old patriarchs knew about the death of the flesh or the little death. They were not conversant with the big death or the death of self, the vanquishing of the ego.

6. This is what Jesus meant when He said, "If any man will come after me, let him deny himself and take up his cross and follow me" (Matt. 16:24).

7. Paul chimed in when he said, "Therefore, if any man be in Christ, he is a new creature: old things are passed away; behold, all things are become new" (II Cor. 5:17).

8. Therefore, every day that we live in this suitcase called flesh, we must take the liberty to die a little here and there that we might live abundantly in Jesus. "For to live is Christ and to die is gain" (Phil 1:29).

9. Yes, your mortality might be precious to your carnal man, but remember, it is a faithful saying, "For if we die with Him, we shall also live with Him (Romans 6:8)."

10. If you really want to know Him, all about Him, you must be willing to accept His horrible death. The man of God wrote, "I am crucified with Christ: nevertheless, I live; yet not I, but Christ liveth in me (Gal. 2:20)." He lives in me to make, a Resurrection Revelation.

CONCLUSION - I want to know Him personally. I need to know Him intimately. I've got to know His voice. I'm pleading to know His vision. I'm dying to know His will.

I'm praying to know His glory that I might attain my "blessed hope," the resurrection of the dead and life in the world to come.

So take my house…Take my car…Take my money…Take my family…Take my hurts…Take my angers…Take my envies…Take everything that I value the most. Put them in one big pile and access my earthly wealth. I'll throw it all away that I might know the King of Kings and the Lord of Lords intimately.

I know what Philip meant when he said, "Show us the Father and it sufficeth us" (John 14:8). I've decided Lord, any way you bless me…any way you deliver me out of this mess…anyway you reveal yourself to me…anyway you use me…any way you allow me to know you, I'll be satisfied. Great God, any glimpse of glory you acquaint me with; will make my cup overflow with love.

Show me your joy…show me your peace…show me your hope…show me your truth…show me your grace…show me your loving kindness and your tender mercies, that I might know you for myself. ~ January 2, 2005

CHAPTER 2

FAITH

Your Labor is Not in Vain	42
After the Rain	45
There's No Place Like Home	50
The Urgency of Now	61
Ten Reasons To Be Thankful	69
Lost and Found	79
I Feel Like Bustin' Loose	82

Your Labor is Not in Vain

One of the most difficult things we face in life is solitude. From the beginning, God saw that Adam needed a companion and so He created Eve. No one likes being alone. We go to great lengths to fit in. We all want to belong to someone or something. Many people will sacrifice their integrity or compromise their beliefs to be accepted by the crowd.

When we are faced with dilemmas of conscience, we often cringe at the thought of being singled out for our beliefs. We want to stand up for what we think is right. But if standing for the "right" alienates us from those closest to us or those we esteem, we often wilt away. Some people have such a strong desire to be acknowledged with the majority that they concede their very souls to please the mob. Popularity, it seems, is more relevant than dignity. That's the way of the world, but not the way of Christ.

As He sat upon the Mount of Olives, Jesus warned His disciples of the conditions of the last age. He told them about wars and their awful rumors, civil unrest and social upheaval. He explained to them that many would be deceived and offended. Because of sin the bank vaults of brotherhood and fellowship would be bankrupt. Yet, He encouraged them. The Lord declared, "But he that shall endure unto the end, the same shall be saved." (Matt. 24:13)

It takes intestinal fortitude to take an unpopular stand. The tide of public opinion polls smash against those who will not compromise their principles. Many who have started out in the right direction have been knocked off course by the cries of the throng. Ask Pontius Pilate.

Standing firm on what you believe in is noble, yet expensive. John Brown hung at Harper's Ferry for his stand. It cost Lincoln his life. Mahatma Gandhi was butchered for his stand. Malcolm X paid for his stand against Elijah Muhammad with his life. Martin King said, "If you don't stand for something, you will fall for anything," and then paid the ultimate price for standing. Jesus the Christ bucked tradition, ignored public opinion, rebuked the enemy and paid for it with His precious blood. Thomas Browne wrote, "Where life is more terrible than death, it is then the truest valor to dare to live."[8]

A controversial little man named Paul told the church at Ephesus to arm themselves with God so that when the day of conflict arrives, they would be able to endure the tribulation, having done everything necessary to stand. He told the Christians at Galatia to continue to sow good seeds even if you don't see immediate results. "And let us not be weary in well doing; for in due season, we shall reap if we faint not." (Gal. 6:19)

To you who have done your best to further the cause of brotherhood, only to have your efforts ridiculed, belittled and criticized by the very people you have tried to elevate, the words of the Apostle Peter might bring some comfort. "But how is it to your credit if you receive a beating for doing wrong and endure it? But if you suffer for doing good and endure it, this is commendable before God" 1 Peter 2:20 NIV)

~ October 22, 2003

---

[8] Douglas, C. N., *Forty Thousand Quotations*, 1917

After the Rain
2 Samuel 23:4

TEXT: *4And he shall be as the light of the morning, when the sun riseth, even a morning without clouds; as the tender grass springing out of the earth by clear shining after rain.*

As King David approached the end of his life around 1018 BC, he reflected upon the beautiful way God used him. His testimony was that his experiences had blessed him. His majestic Psalms were inspired by the very spirit of the Living God. He conceded that his words were actually God's words. In David's many conquests, the LORD received honor and glory.

As a kingly or royal priest, David was obligated to rule over Israel and Judah in praise, worship and reverence unto God. For thousands of years His unforgettable songs of praise and worship have encouraged broken hearted people to, "lift their eyes to the hills from whence cometh our help, knowing that all our help cometh from the Lord who created the Heavens and the earth" (Psalm 121:1).

In 2nd Samuel 23 is a recording of King David's final speech. His words translated from David Sterns complete Hebrew Bible are passionate, profound and strikingly beautiful. In reference to the Mashiach (Messiah), David declares, "A ruler over people must be upright, ruling in fear of God; like the morning light at sunrise on a cloudless day that makes the grass on the earth sparkle after a rain."[9]

I. David could savor these powerful words of praise because there had been so much rain in his life. When Saul, a man he loved like a father, became violently jealous, David had to run for his life, sometimes hiding in dark caves for safety. Even as king, David's flesh was weak causing him to engineer the death of a friend in order to sleep with his wife. His destruction of another man's family led to chaos in his own family. Incest, bloody revenge and finally a coup against the throne by his third son Absalom (whose death David mourned for years) was the product of the king's corruption.

II. This great father of the faith was well acquainted with the storms of life. He was witness to the uncertainty that accompanies storms, the disruption that attaches itself to storms. He managed to hold on through the

---

[9] Stern, David H., *Complete Jewish Bible*, 1998

winds of change, the rains of adversity, the thunder and lightning of sickness and disease. He kept the faith through floods of fears and anxieties. Even the great flood in Noah's day ended after 40 days. The dark clouds of loneliness, betrayal and abandonment encompassed him but David encouraged himself… "this too shall pass" and "it is well with my soul". No wonder he could walk through the valley of the shadow of death without fear or trepidation.

III. In life, it seems as if storms never end. If you are not coming out of one, you are probably going into one; life is full of cycles. The vicissitudes of life often leave us feeling empty and devoid. We take one step forward only to be blown back two. Bumped and bruised through life, we lose hope in the future and ourselves. Rather than surrender Paul manages to encourage… "Let us not be weary in well doing: for in due season we shall reap if we faint not" (Gal 6:9 KJV). In other words if your storm doesn't kill you it will only make you stronger and wiser. How would the trees grow if the winds did not rock them from side to side every now and then?

IV. I'm glad David knew something about the promises of God. He knew that even trouble don't last always. If you don't know that God is true to His Word you will lose hope when in life's storms. He knew that the Mashiach promised to Eve in the Garden of Eden and promised to the patriarchs of Israel, was indeed the same one God promised him. God told David...Thine house and thy kingdom shall be established forever before thee: thy throne shall be established forever (2 Samuel 7:16 KJV). He reassured the king of Israel… Sit thou on my right hand while I make thy enemies thy footstool (Matt 22:44).

No wonder he could rejoice in the face of death. His root and offspring is the Bright and Morning Star. David could see the breaking of a brand new day. David realized that after weeping all night, joy would come in the morning. No matter how hard it rains in your life, remember that eventually, storm systems roll away, replaced by sunshine...in the morning. And when the brightness of the Son illuminates the earth; that which seemed dead is resurrected. Tender green shoots spring from the ground shouting, 'Hallelujah,' and you can behold the beauty of my sweet Savior...after the rain. I believe this occasioned Josiah Allwood to write, "Oh they tell me of a home far beyond the sky. They tell me of a home far, far, away. Yes they tell me of a home where no storm clouds rise. Oh they tell me of an uncloudy day.[10]

~ August 7, 2006

---

[10] Allwood, Josiah K., "*Uncloudy Day*", 1880

There's No Place Like Home
Luke 15:18-20 & 24

TEXT - *I will arise and go to my father, and will say unto him, father, I have sinned against heaven, and before thee, and am no more worthy to be called thy son: make me one of thy hired servants, And he arose and came to his father. But when he was yet a great way off, his father saw him and had compassion and ran, and fell on his neck, and kissed him ... For this, my son, was dead and is alive again, he was lost, and is found. And they began to be merry.*

EXPOSITION - From the previous chapter we find Jesus in 28AD, at the home of a Pharisee having dinner, when he hears the mumbling and murmuring of members of the Sanhedrin Council. They were upset because he received publicans and sinners at the dinner table with him. These Jewish leaders would never associate with such social outcast. This display of disapproval prompted Jesus to deliver a trilogy or three related parables specifically concerned with lost souls being brought into the kingdom of heaven.

First he talks about the lost sheep and the joy in heaven over its return. Then the lost coin which the woman turned her house upside down to find. And finally, the lost son, one of the most cherished parables in scripture. Jesus used parables to give simple meaning to sometimes-complicated truths. Parable is from the Greek word parabola (an earthly story with heavenly implications).

EXEGESIS - Jesus declared that a certain man had two sons. The firstborn or the older son was industrious. He was a hard worker. He was obedient and diligent. The older son knew his role in the family and made great strides to carry out his father's wishes. In the Jewish family tradition of ancient Israel, possessions were passed on to the living sons of a father, but the first born or eldest son received a double portion. This incentive made the older son more inclined to be thrifty, dependable and submissive. The more wealth he reaped for his father, the greater his personal fortune grew. This elder of the two sons was patiently waiting for the day when his faithfulness would turn into inheritance.

The man also had a younger son. The younger son found himself in the shadow of his big brother. The younger son was constantly second fiddle to his brother, relegated to bit parts and minor roles. He longed for something new and exciting. He was tired of being the "low man on the totem pole". He thought if I could get away from here my life would be better. I'm a nobody here, but maybe in a new place, a different venue, I can be somebody important. I can be a star.

TEARS OF A CLOWN

I. The younger brother went to his father and asked for an advance on his inheritance or one third of his father's wealth. His father gave him his portion and the younger brother packed his bags and hit the road. He went looking for the better place. He traveled until he reached a far country.

1. In the far country he was an overnight sensation. The people loved him. No longer in his brother's shadow he was his own man. He could make his own decisions.

2. He decided that the best way to be popular was to throw a party. At the party he had the best food, the best music, and the best champagne money could buy. His party was off the hook. Many said it was the social event of the season and all the ladies loved him. He had a high approval rating in all the exit polls.

3. In order to stay popular he had to throw more parties. Overdone, gaudy, elaborate spectacles that cost more money. What seemed like an endless supply of cash was dwindling fast?

4. He began to notice that as his cash dwindled, so did his popularity. The homeboys he used to run with no longer had time for him. The ladies who once showered him with love and affections were too busy getting cozy with the new high roller, to pay him any attention.

5. The young brother was broke. He had wasted his substance with riotous living, miscalculated living, uncontrolled and unpurposed living.

6. Now the bottom drops out the barrel. Not only was he broke but a famine devastated the land. The food supply was all but gone. Jobs were scarce. Money was tight. The so-called friends he thought he once had, turned a deaf ear to his pleas for help.

7. At his wits end, he stumbled upon a man who had a herd of swine. Desperate, the younger brother asked to feed the hogs, in exchange for some of the cornhusk that they ate.

8. The younger brother had fallen to an all-time low in life. For it is considered sacrilege, even apostasy, for a Jew to have any contact with swine or those who herd

them. In the eyes of the temple priest, he was ceremoniously unclean.

9. Then one day as he fed the pigs he received a revelation. He came to his senses. He thought to himself; how many hired servants of my fathers have bread enough and to spare, and I perish with hunger?

10. Living with hogs will humble you. Living in a hog pen can bring out some character in you that you never knew was there. Living in a hog pen will make you count your blessings. Living in a hog pen will make you appreciate the little things in life. Living in a hog pen will make you smell the filth of your own excessive behavior.

11. The younger brother rose up and declared, "I'm going home and tell my father that I have sinned against heaven, and before thee. I'm not worthy to be thy son, just make me a servant. Make me a hired hand and I'll work faithfully in your fields."

12. With his statement of repentance prepared, the reckless, wasteful son went back to his place of birth, back to his father's home. While he was yet a long way from the house, his father (who had been waiting for the son to return everyday) saw him in the distance. He did not have to

guess who it was or take a second look. He knew it was his youngest boy.

13. The father's heart burst with joy. He ran across the fields and put his arms around the son and greeted him with a welcome kiss.

14. The younger son tried to apologize for the error of his ways but the happy father over looked the past. He told his servants bring the best robe and put it on him, and put a ring on his hand, and shoes on his feet. Then kill the fatted calf and let's eat, drink and be merry. For this my son was dead, and is alive again; he was lost, and is found.

II. In our lives we are often blessed by Jehovah God with riches of life, health, wealth and intellect. Unappreciative and unsatisfied, we take what he has bestowed upon us for granted and wonder off to a far country. We wander about looking for an imaginary greener pasture.

1. We get in the fast lane, the big time, the easy street, the foot loose and the fancy-free. We find ourselves in Another World on Sun Set Beach. We try to keep up with The Young

and Restless. We want to be seen with the Bold and Beautiful, As the World Turns. Loving, All My Children, we forget the Guiding Light. We forget that we have only One Life to Live. We take Law and Order for granted. Some of us end up spending the Days of Our Lives in General Hospital or the ER room of Chicago Hope, or on the West Wing of Comic View, praying for an American Idol to make us the next Top Model.

2. In a far off country … Friends are plentiful and favors are frequent. Your popularity is ever increasing. Yes, out there in the far country seems the place to be because the world is your stage and you're the star of the show. You've got top billing now. You're big ballin', shot callin' bling blinging and cha chinging. in the far country.

3. But suddenly, when you least expect it, when you think you can make it without God's help in the far country, somebody flips the script. Somebody pulls the plug. Somebody cuts off the power. Somebody

writes you a bad check in the far country.

4. Your pockets turn up empty. You're so broke you can't pay attention. The fast lane moves at a snail's pace. The favors are inconsistent. So called friends don't call you any more, except to ask you to return whatever you borrowed from them. Those who put you on the pedestal are chopping you down. Those who laughed with you are now laughing at and about you. If you think it's lonely at the top, its solitary confinement at the bottom.

5. Nobody loves a loser. Nobody wants you when you're down and out. The grass you thought was so green on the other side turns out to be artificial turf. It turns out to be dried up and full of weeds. No, the far country is not the place you thought it would be.

6. When you turn your back on Jesus, you find yourself working in a hog pen of sin. Doing things you normally would not do, going places you know you should avoid. There is envy in the hog pen. There is hate, lies, lust, corruption, gossip,

addiction, scandals and so much pain in the hog pen of life.

7. I'm so glad that God instills in each of us a sense of oughtness that makes you say at your lowest point,

"I don't have to live like this. I don't have to wallow in the filth of sin. I'm wondrously and marvelously made in the image of Elohim. I don't have to dwell in the gutters. I don't have to continue to live in shame." David prayed, "O God, wash me thoroughly from mine iniquity, and cleanse me from my sin ... Purge me with hyssop, and I shall be clean: wash me and I shall be whiter than snow."

8. Lord save me! Lord cleanse me! Lord change me! Renew my faith, restore my joy, create in me a clean heart, and renew in me a right spirit... Charles Wesley so aptly prayed, "Father I stretch my hand to thee, no other help, I know. If thou withdraw thyself from me wherever shall I go?"[11]

TRANSITION - *There is no place like home*, no how no way, nowhere - no place like home... I'm so glad; "That if our

---

[11] Wesley, Charles, "*A Collection of Psalms and Hymns*", 1741

earthly tabernacle were dissolved, we have a building of God, a house not made with hands, eternal in the heavens" (2 Cor 5:1).

III. That lets me know that no matter how big or pretty or costly a house may be, home is more than a house. Home is not constructed with brick and mortar. Home means more than beds and chairs. Home is where your heart is.

1. Home is where your mind is. Home is where your soul is. I'm so glad that this old mean world is not my home. I'm but a pilgrim passing through this barren land. I'm looking for the city with foundations, whose architect and builder is God (Heb. 11:10).

2. One glad morning when this life is over, I'll fly away. I'm going home to be with the Lord. I've already made a reservation. My ticket is secure. I've already got a place to stay. I've established residence there for Jesus said, "In my Father's house are many mansions ... I go to prepare a place for you that where I am, ye may be also (John 14:2)." Aren't you glad that won't

have to pay rent or borrow money or secure a fixed interest rate when you go home ... Why? Because Jesus paid it all far in advance.

CONCLUSION - One day, my Heavenly Father will meet me coming up the King's Highway. God will run out to me and take me in his everlasting arms and kiss all my tears away. He's going to dress me in the finest robe, put a gold ring on my finger. I'll put on my new shoes and run, dance and shout all over God's heaven. Than shall I hear his mighty voice say to the angels, "Rejoice, and be glad; for this is my son who was dead and is alive again." He was lost and is found. He was sick, now he is healed. He was damned, now delivered. He was cursed, now he is blessed. He was cast out, now he is received. He was dismissed, but now he is welcomed in the Kingdom of Heaven.

~ June 18, 2006

The Urgency of Now
Hebrews 11:1

TEXT: *Now faith is the substance of things hoped for, the evidence of things not seen.*

INTRODUCTION - On April 22, 2008 reporters in New Orleans asked President George W. Bush if the United States economy is in a recession. Even though the nation's Gross Domestic Product has diminished significantly over the last two years; the President still tows the company line saying; Our economy is fine, we're only experiencing a slowdown. Obviously our chief executive is out of touch with 80% of the citizens of this country.

Mr. Bush is clearly disconnected from the reality that people in this real world are suffering great hardships. Maybe he can't relate to the pain of the masses because he is so insulated by power, position, and wealth. I'll be the first to admit that I greatly appreciate the economic stimulus check the government is distributing. The real fact of the matter is that the stimulus will help pay some bills that need immediate attention and put some money back into the struggling economy but it won't decrease the cost of a gallon of gas.

In January 2007, Congress raised the minimum wage to $6.15. This week the cost of a gallon of unleaded regular gas topped $3.99. So now the youngest and the poorest workers don't make enough money per hour to afford two gallons of gas. Unemployed and laid off shift workers are in danger of their unemployment benefits being cut off. The incredible cost of gas is directly tied to the cost of food increasing almost 20% in the last two years.

Around the globe people in third world countries are fighting for basic foods we take for granted every day! Corn, rice wheat, eggs, and bread are priced 25% higher than market value 18 months ago in Haiti, Asia, Egypt, and West Africa. I believe Mr. Bush missed the morning briefing in the West Wing. Someone forgot to tell him, Mr. President we're in the midst of a deep recession. Indeed a famine has struck our land. This is no false alarm. This emergency is real. This house is on fire and the roof is about to collapse.

Money alone won't cure a housing crisis in which middle class families face foreclosure, repossession, and out of control adjustable rate mortgages.

Increased troop levels alone will not bring peace to Iraq and bring our troops home from Afghanistan. Troops cannot make neighbors love one another and share power… equitability.

Mandatory health insurance alone will not cover the 50 million Americans who cannot afford to visit the doctor and often suffer from self-diagnosis in the world's most profitable health-care system.

The construction of more maximum security prisons (alone) will not decrease the soaring crime rate or diminish gang violence. Enacting free trade agreements might stimulate the global economy but what about replacing the jobs lost around here?

Our nation is in desperation for real change. The land is sick and needs to be healed. The Apostle Paul said it best… "The whole creation groaneth and travaileth in pain together until now (Rom. 8:22)." In order to survive until the Lord comes back for his *ekklesia*, (the body of baptized believers) we must acknowledge the "*Urgency of Now*".

EXPOSITION - The author of this letter to Messianic Jews, dated prior to the destruction of the temple at Jerusalem in 70 AD, hoped to persuade a colony of Jewish Christians to maintain their faith in the coming Messiah. This first century church was waiting for Jesus to return soon. Many of them grew impatient and weary under the barrage of persecutions they received at the hands of Roman authorities in Italy. The author wanted his readers to stand fast in their faith rather than return to the oppression of ritualistic Judaism. So the writer begins a laundry list of Christ "betters" when compared to angels, Moses the lawgiver, Joshua the warrior, Aaron the high priest, the prophets and Judaism as a whole.

In chapter 11 the author calls the roll of some of the great heroes and champions of faith. They endured great adversity, sufferings, trial and tribulations and yet they were able to overcome tragic situations by their unwavering urgent faith. The author does not attempt here to give us a technical definition of what faith is;

instead he wants us to know how faith works.

EXEGESIS - Now (*Chronos* or chronological time deals with the past, present, or future. *Kairos* or divine order; God's perfect will, now reflects the moment before us that we must somehow live with under the present circumstances). <u>Faith</u> (trust, from the Greek word *pistis*) <u>is the substance</u> (being confident from the Greek word *upostasis* meaning that which stands under and allows us title or deed to the property) <u>of things</u> (stuff and events) <u>hoped for</u> (expected, anticipated) <u>the evidence</u> (what gives present reality to what we hope) <u>of things not seen</u> (in earth or in the natural). Essentially faith is believing what you see without seeing what you believe. Faith is proof without physiology.

I.   The Urgency of now is not <u>rational</u> until it is experienced.

    1. I can tell you all day long that the Lord will make a way out of no way but until you find yourself in deep trouble painted into a corner with no options or alternatives you won't believe what I say until you experience what I've been through.

2. I can admonish you to have faith but the rational mind has trouble accepting what it cannot see, smell or touch.
3. That's due to the fact that faith is not rational to us. Faith is not innate nor is it contrived. It's not incarnate or built into our psyche. In other words we're not born with faith.
4. Faith is something that grows in you. Faith must be built and established on a foundation of experience.
5. Many of us are going through hell in our lives. We are catching it from all angles and every side. The adversary is throwing everything at us but the kitchen sink and yet we continue to hold out and hold on and hold up the blood stained banner.
6. It was our faith in God that kept us through slavery – Jim Crow – The Civil Rights movement and whenever we wanted to let go. We acquire this faith by hearing the matriarchs, patriarchs, and seasoned saints witness to the goodness of God. We attach ourselves to this

faith through the testimony of the righteous. We embrace this faith through the *kerygma*, the apostolic preaching of the gospel. So then faith cometh by hearing and hearing by the word of God (Rom. 10:17).

7. Faith makes no sense when you really think about it and therein lies it power. For faith pulls reality out of impossibility.

8. Jesus said, "If you have faith as a grain of mustard seed, ye shall say unto this mountain be thou removed to yonder place and it shall remove and nothing shall be impossible unto you" (Matt. 17:20). *The Urgency of now is not recognized until it is challenged.*

II. The Urgency of now is not real until it is tested and tried. Sickness, loss, injury, disaster, bankruptcy, and death, push us to the breaking point.

1. Jesus was tested in the wilderness by Satan and tried in Gethsemane by death.

2. "Blessed is the man that endureth temptation; for when he is tried, he shall receive the crown of life.

For the just shall live by faith" (Heb. 10:38). Paul declared not that I speak in respect of want; for I have learned, "in whatsoever state I am, there to be content" (Phil. 4:11). Urgency = <u>Now</u> spelled backward is <u>Won</u>! Jesus won victory over the world for you and me.

CONCLUSION - "For whatsoever is born of God overcometh the world; this is the victory that overcometh the world, even our faith" (1 John 5:4). The prince of the air bombards our minds with news of gloom, doom, and despair. These dark reports make many of us want to throw in the towel. There is a battle going on in our minds. Yet by faith we will prevail and overcome. By faith we will prevail… Victorious! Triumphant! Undefeated!

~ April 6, 2008

Ten Reasons To Be Thankful
I Thessalonians 5:16-18

TEXT - *Rejoice evermore. Pray without ceasing. In everything give thanks: for this is the will of God in Christ concerning you.*

EXPOSITION - Paul concluded his first missionary journey at Antioch in 48AD. A year later he was a key figure in the Apostolic Council that met at Jerusalem. Departing from the holy city with Silas, he began his second missionary journey by traveling through Syria, Cilicia, Derbe and Lystra where he met Timothy. After being jailed in the Macedonian province of Philippi, Paul made it to Thessalonica in 50AD. The prophet stayed in the home of a believer named Jason, but only for three weeks. It seems that a riot broke out among the Jews because of the multitudes that were being won to a belief in Jesus as the Christ of God.

The Jewish elders were envious of the drawing power of the preached gospel and conspired to destroy Paul and Silas. The prophets escaped the city unscathed and fled to Berea, 50 miles to the west. The Jewish elders found out where these men (who had turned the world upside down) were hiding and stirred up trouble there. Run out of town again, Paul fled to Athens, 200 miles south.

INTRODUCTION - In Athens, Paul stood before the philosophers on Mars Hill and delivered his great Aeropagus speech. Always the itinerant preacher, Paul moved on to Corinth where Timothy met him. The young evangelist reported that the church which the apostle organized only a few months earlier was faithfully enduring persecutions. But there was some concern about those who had died for the faith before the Lord's second coming. To this end Paul wrote the earliest extant or the first written New Testament book. He did this to expound upon the "*parousia*" or the day of the Lord; to confirm young converts in the elementary truths of the gospel; And, to condition them to pursue holy living.

TRANSITION - In chapter five Paul begins to conclude his letter with fifteen beautiful exhortations.

I. Paul's eighth exhortation to the Thessalonian church is ...
   Rejoice evermore. Greek (chairo) meaning happy, glad, joyous (pantote) meaning continuous, always, perpetual
   1. Our joy is in the God of our salvation. His joy is complete joy; fulfilling joy; holistic joy; sustaining joy.

2. The joy we find in the world never last very long...
   a. The joy of winning the game only last until the next game.
   b. The joy of breaking a record only last until that record is broken.
   c. The joy of getting high or drunk only last until you wake up sick and stinky the next morning.
   d. The joy of fornication only last until you find out somebody's got AIDS.
   e. The joy of big money only last until there's little left.
   f. The joy of being famous only last until you are forgotten.
   g. The joy of sneaking around only last until you get caught.
3. But Paul knew about a joy that would keep him through beatings and burdens, depression and doubts, grief and guilt, sickness and sorrow, tragedy and turmoil. He told the Philippian church: Rejoice in the Lord always: and again I say, rejoice (Phil. 4:4).
4. Those of us who have been in the produce section of God's supermarket know that joy is a fruit of the spirit.

5. That's why I can smile in the midst of frowns. I can be calm among cantankerous people. I can be content in the proximity of confusion. Nehemiah declared ... "Neither be ye sorry; for the joy of the Lord is your strength (Neh. 8:10)". Paul said, "Not that I speak in respect of want: for I have learned, in whatsoever state I am, there with to be content (Phil. 14:11)."
6. Even when your heart is heaviest and your eyes can't hold back the tears remember, weeping may endure for a night, but joy cometh in the morning
7. Shirley Caesar once declared: This joy that I have the world did not give it to me. The world didn't give it. The world can't take it away.[12]

II. The ninth exhortation is ... Pray without ceasing. Greek (pros-yoo-khom-ahee) prostrate, supplicate, and worship (ad-ee-ab-ipe-tos) uninterruptedly, without omission.

---

[12] Caesar, Shirley, *"This Joy I Have"*, Artemis Gospel, 1999

1. This exhortation is emphasizing the habit rather than acts of prayer. We all can act a prayer at the dinner table; when called upon, or before we fall asleep at night.
2. Unceasing prayer was needed to secure Peter's release from Herod's prison
3. It was prayer without ceasing that caused our Savior to sweat as it were great drops of blood falling down to the ground
4. Many of us pray until we get what we want and then we cease to pray, until we want something else.
5. This does not mean that we should spend our entire lives at prayer, that is not logical
6. But, we should spend our lives <u>in</u> prayer. In a spirit of prayer. In a posture of prayer. We must learn how to put our souls on automatic pilot and pray anywhere and everywhere we go.
7. Pray on your job. In your home. At school. On the bus. In your car. At the doctor's office. At church. You ought to take the Lord with you everywhere you go.

TEN REASONS TO BE THANKFUL

8. In order to rejoice evermore, you must learn how to pray without ceasing.
9. Some of us complain that we don't have this or that as if God messed up our order. Don't you know that my God is never late? Have you not heard? He might not get there when you want him, but he is always right on time!
10. You have not because you ask not. Jesus said: "All things whatsoever you ask in prayer, believing, ye shall receive" (Matt. 21:22).

TRANSITION - David knew this when he said: "Evening and morning and noon will I pray and cry aloud, and he shall hear my voice" (Psa. 55:17).

III. The apostles tenth exhortation is paramount to our walk with God ... In everything give thanks, for this is the will of God in Christ concerning you. Greek (eucharisteo) to be grateful, show gratitude. If I had ten thousand tongues I could never thank God enough for all his manifold blessings so I just want to highlight…Ten Reasons to be thankful.

1. <u>The little things that I might take for granted</u>. Sunshine, moonlight the twinkle of the stars, the

song of the cricket, the wing span of an eagle, oxygen, grass, dirt, flowers, trees, saliva in my mouth and hairs that line my nose. "The earth is the Lords and the fullness therefore"(Psa. 24:1).

2. <u>My Health</u>. The ability to get out of bed under my own strength. The ability to wash and dress myself, vision, hearing, smelling, tasting, feeling, hands that hold, feet that walk, knees that bend, functional liver, lungs stomach, kidneys pancreas, thyroid, colon, intestines and a heart that still pumps. "I will praise thee for I am fearfully and wonderfully made" (Psa. 139:14).

3. <u>My earthly disappointments</u>. Setbacks, bad breaks, malfunctions, my car breaking down, my lights being cut off, eviction notice, bad credit, sorry husband, no good wife, lazy children, backstabbing friends, mean enemies, tears in the night, stiffness in the morning, pain in my body, sorrow, death, grief, the things that I wanted that you didn't want me to have, this heavy cross that I must carry in the heat of the day. "My grace is sufficient for thee: for my strength is made perfect in weakness" (2nd Cor. 12:9).

4. <u>The church.</u> My Schechem, my Shiloh, my Bethel, my sanctuary, my tabernacle, my pavilion, that which my Savior built that nothing, not even the gates of hell can destroy; The Ecclesia, the called out assembly of new born, baptized believers. The saved, sanctified, holy ghost filled, fire baptized. "How good and how pleasant it, is for brethren to dwell together in unity (Psa. 133:1)". Jesus said, "Upon this Rock I will build my church" (Matt. 16:18).

5. <u>Family.</u> Husband, wife, son, daughter, mother, father, sister, brother, aunt, uncle, cousins, niece, nephew, grandson, granddaughter, godparents, godchildren, close friends (The family that prays together).

6. <u>Provisions</u>. Electricity, running water, heat, air conditioning, toilet, job, money, house, car, clothes, food, sleep, TV-cable, furniture, and all the other stuff that God has loaned me. Songwriter wrote: Though you may not drive a great big Cadillac, gangster white walls, TV antenna in the back. You may not have a car at all, but remember brother and sister you can still stand tall. Just be thankful for

what you've got.[13]

7. <u>Spiritual Wonders</u>. Forgiveness, mercy, grace, tenderness, compassion, redemption, reconciliation, justification, adaptation, power, love, peace, long-suffering, gentleness, goodness, faith, meekness, temperance against which there is no law. (What God has for me it is for me).

8. <u>Life</u>. Earth's most precious gift. Something that only God can give and only God can take away. And not just any old life but an abundance of life. New life, life running through my veins. Life with real hope and real meaning… "If any man be in Christ, he is a new creature: old things are passed away; behold, all things are become new" (2nd Corinth 5:17).

9. <u>My Salvation</u>. I did nothing to deserve it. I was slow to embrace it. I thought I could inherit if from my mother but she couldn't pass it to me. I tried to buy it but it wasn't for sale. I tried to study it but it was unsearchable. Finally I just asked for it and it was

---

[13] DeVaughn, William, "*Be Thankful for What You Got*", Omega Sound, 1972

freely given. I would not trade anything for my salvation. "For God sent not his Son into the world to condemn the world; but that the world through him might be saved" (John 3:17).

CONCLUSION - The number one blessing I have to be thankful for is Jesus the Christ. From the beginning ... His virgin birth ... His earthly ministry ... His death on the cross, burial in the grave and resurrection on the third day is my blessed hope! His ascension is evidence of a task successfully completed. For these and countless other reasons I am forever thankful.

~ November 22, 2003

Lost and Found

As he came to the conclusion of another powerful sermon, my father told the story of a lost little boy...

It seems that the four-year-old slipped out the back door, while his mother was distracted with household chores. He made his way across the backyard, through the neighbor's yard and out onto the adjacent street. "So this is what the world looks like," the child thought to himself. He had often wondered why mommy wouldn't let him leave the yard. He was four years old, tall for his age. "I'm not afraid of anything," he assured himself.

He walked down a long street. A lady working in her yard stopped and smiled at him. He waved and skipped along the sidewalk. He turned the corner and went down another street. There he spotted men sitting around a makeshift table playing checkers. He stopped for a moment to watch. One of the men looked up from the board and asked the child, "Do you want to play?" He shook his head and ran down the street.

He saw children playing on the swings and so he crossed the street. He blended right in with the gang. They slid down the sliding boards. They climbed the monkey bars, went up and down on the seesaw and dug in the sandbox.

A nice little girl brought a ball to the playground. He learned to play kickball and dodge ball. He was having so much fun that he didn't even think about the sun setting behind him. The other children heard their mothers call and, one by one, they all ran home. The little boy continued to play until he realized that he was alone. All of his wonderful new playmates had abandoned him. The bright and friendly park suddenly became dark and scary.

The little boy was hungry, tired and lonely. He wanted to see mommy. He sat in the swing and began to cry. A few moments later, a police officer on patrol spotted a solitary figure on the swing. He got out of his car and approached the child. He asked the little boy what was wrong. Through broken sobs, the child cried, "I want my mommy!"

The officer asked for an address, the child didn't know. "How about your phone number?" The little boy shook his head. "What's your parent's name?" The lad replied, "Mommy and Daddy."

The officer offered the child his hand and led him to his patrol car. He drove slowly through the neighborhood trying to find the child's home. "Does this street look familiar?" Over and over again the child replied, "No." Then the officer replied, "What's close to your house?" The little boy thought for a moment, images racing through his head. Finally a memory stuck in his mind. He told the officer, "There's a place close to my house with a big cross on top. If I can get to the cross, I will find my way home."

So many of us have drifted away from home looking for vainglory, worldly treasures and monetary pleasure only to end up abandoned, empty, lonely and lost. But be encouraged. Don't give up. God is waiting for your return with open arms, the same way they were opened to you 2000 years ago on the cross.

~ July 24, 2004

I FEEL LIKE BUSTIN LOOSE
JOHN 11:43 – 44 KJV

TEXT - *And when He thus had spoken, He cried with a loud voice, Lazarus, come forth. And he that was dead came forth, bound hand and foot with grave clothes: and his face bound about with a napkin. Jesus saith unto them, "Loose him, and let him go."*

TITLE – I FEEL LIKE BUSTIN LOOSE

EXPOSITION – As the winter began to lose its grip early in AD 30, Jesus was a fugitive on the lam. Late in AD 29 He had a heated debate with the Jewish leadership in Jerusalem at the Feast of Dedication. When He told them that He was one with the Father the mob took up stones to kill Him. Somehow He managed to avoid their wrath, walking through the midst of them unnoticed. Now in what proved to be a bold move, He departed from the Trans-Jordan region and returned to the outskirts of Jerusalem. He was headed to Bethany to the home of His beloved friends, Lazarus, Martha, and Miriam or Mary. He had shared many pleasant meals with this family and their home was a place of fellowship and refuge.

I. As He approached the village a courier met Him with an urgent message from Martha and Mary. In essence the message said, "Lord, hurry and come. Your great friend Lazarus is gravely ill."

   1. The disciples anticipated that the Lord would take immediate action and quickly make the two mile hike to Bethany to restore His dear friend. Instead He sat down, leaned back and said, "This sickness will not end in death. No, it's for the glory of God, so that the son of God may receive glory through it."

   2. The disciples were puzzled, for they had seen Him move with haste to perform miracles and to minister to strangers. Now His dear friend is very sick and his family is seeking divine intervention, yet he doesn't move.

   3. Its' two days later before Jesus breaks camp and says, "Let's go back to Judea." Despite their warnings of warrants for His arrest Jesus headed for Bethany in Judea. The Lord left Judea several months earlier after finding out that John the Baptizer had been apprehended and subsequently

beheaded by the Idumean King Herod Agrippa. Word had it that Jesus was next, so He left Judea and avoided Perea because these territories were ruled by Herod Agrippa at the bidding of Tiberius Caesar.

1. Jesus could not risk being stoned to death by the Jews or beheaded by Herod or ambushed by paid assassins. In order to fulfill His own prophesy He had to die on an execution state. During His triumphal entry into Jerusalem, Jesus was heard to say, "If I be lifted up from the earth I'll draw all men unto me" (John 12:32).

2. Before they headed to Bethany, Jesus explained to the disciples that Lazarus was dead. He was glad for this opportunity, for Lazarus' death would be used for the disciple's edification and God's glorification.

III. As Jesus and His entourage approached Lazarus home, word of His pending arrival reached Martha who immediately ran out to confront the Lord with her personal medical assessment.

1. She felt the need to blame somebody. She said, "Lord, if you would have been here my brother would not have died". Then in an almost cynical tone she added, "But I know, that even now, whatsoever thou will ask of God,

God will give you." In other words you could have spoken a word from wherever you were and God would have healed our brother.

2. If you listen closely you can hear the biting sarcasm in Martha's voice. It's the sound of disappointment, defeat, and doubt. She's thinking within herself, "We wouldn't be here if He would have come when we called Him." Like many of us Martha forgot that you can't hurry God. You can't microwave God. God does what He wants to, where He wants to, whenever He wants to.

3. To fully comprehend Martha's hurt you must understand how displaced a woman was in the very sexist, male dominated society of first century Palestine.

4. As evidenced by the parable of the prodigal son the property of a father was always split among the man's sons with the oldest receiving the most. Daughters were not included in this division. They were betrothed or promised in a prearranged marriage at an early age by negotiations between two

male elders. This was the case with Mary and Joseph's fathers.

5. Women in this culture owned no property as was the case in the story of Naomi and Ruth. Boaz the male relative secured the continuation of Naomi's husband and son's bloodline, as a kinsman redeemer and then married Ruth.

6. With Lazarus dead there was no male figure in the home. The sisters were at the mercy of the nearest male relative who could have decided to evict them from their home and sell their property without a second thought.

7. Jesus attempted to reassure Martha that Lazarus would rise again. Resigned to the fact that her brother was forever gone in the earth realm, she replied "I know he will rise again at the Resurrection on the last day." Jesus countered her lack of faith with his most magnificent "I am" declaration. He said, "I am the Resurrection and the Life."

8. In saying this He summarizes all the Old Testament doctrines and prophecies and transforms them into one being the logos or the living word. At the same time He confronts Martha's and our fears of death and the grave by declaring His dominion over both. He promised her that whoever trusts in Him will live and never ever die.

TRANSITION - Paul said, "So when this corruptible shall have put on incorruption, and this mortal shall have put on immortality, then shall be brought to pass the saying that is written, Death is swallowed up in victory" (I Corinthians 15:54).

IV. With this new faith Martha returned to the family home where Mary was sitting shiv'ah. Shiv'ah was a seven day period of mourning for Hebrew people. They would not leave the home during this period. Martha secretly told Mary "the Master is come and calleth for thee. She did this because many Jews were at the house and there was an order for his arrest from Caiphas and the Sanhedrin Council.

1. Mary ran out to meet Jesus with the mourner's right behind her thinking she was headed to the grave.

When she saw the Lord she fell at His feet as she had before when she washed His feet with her tears and dried them with her hair. She would later fall at His feet and worship Him when He emerged from the grave on Resurrection morning.

2. Between sobs she repeats what everyone (the disciples, the messenger, the spies and the Jews) were thinking. "Lord if you had been here, my brother would not have died." The rumor had circulated that Jesus' negligence in delaying caused Lazarus untimely death. They all blamed Jesus. This caused him noticeable discomfort. He groaned in the Spirit and asked them, "Where have you buried him?" They said, "Lord come see." And then Jesus (the same man whose victory would ultimately swallow death) wept.

3. They led a very disturbed Jesus to the gravesite He told them to "Take the stone away." Martha's lack of faith emerged. She said to Jesus, "By now his

body must smell, for it has been four days since he died." Jesus wanted everyone to smell the stench of death emanating from Lazarus body so that there would be no doubt that this was his greatest miracle. Others He raised from the dead were just a few hours deceased. Jairus daughter was only a few hours' dead when Jesus raised her. Rigamortis had not set in. Decay had not begun to ravage the body. The Jews had a superstition that the spirit hovered around the body for three days until corruption set in and then took flight. Jesus knew when His friend died. He waited for this moment when there could be no doubt about the magnitude of the miracle. He reminded Martha of the message He had sent back by the courier, that if they trusted they would see the glory of God.

4. When they removed the stone the unmistakable odor of death filled every nostril. At that moment Jesus began to pray out loud to the Father, thanking Him for always hearing Him and proving beyond a shadow of a doubt that the Father sent Him.

5. Then Jesus shouted the dead man's name El'azar! Without delay or hesitation the dead man somehow got

up and emerged from the cave wrapped in strips of linen and his face covered with a cloth. Then Jesus commanded his disciples "Loose Him and let him go!"

I FEEL LIKE BUSTIN' LOOSE

V. I remember a go-go funk band from the Washington metro area called Chuck Brown and the Soul Searchers. In 1982 they scored a disco hit with a song entitled, "*I feel like Bustin Loose.*" The song had a heavy bass line and hard jamming horns in the bridge. Several weeks ago I heard the song on the radio but this time I heard something different. Instead of the bumping bass and blaring horns I heard Chuck sing the lyrics. He said he felt like busting loose from the things which were oppressing him. "*Bustin' Loose* in the evening. *Bustin' Loose* kinda pleasing. Talking bout *bustin' loose. Bustin' loose* in the mean time, *bustin' loose* kinda feel fine. Talking 'bout *bustin' loose. Bustin' loose* when you want to swing. *Bustin' loose* baby do your thing. Give me the bridge now."

1. Sometimes I feel like Chuck Brown. I feel like Lazarus, all tied up. Sometimes the troubles of this world get so cumbersome, *I feel like bustin loose.*
2. We need to trust in Jesus. Instead we get tied up in apathy and we just don't care anymore.
3. We get caught up in bad relationships and we hold on even when we know it's killing us because we believe a bad relationship is better than no relationship at all.
4. We're captured by fear and so we miss our blessing because we're afraid to walk by faith and not by sight.
5. We get trapped by how we look and end up buying everything on the market to make us look more like the stars.
6. We get caught up in gossip and start looking for dirt on everybody else not realizing that our lives are tore up from the floor up.
7. We get pinned down by jealousy because we forget "What God has for me it is for me."

8. We get hung up in pride because we forget that it goes before destruction and a haughty spirit before a fall.
9. We get locked down in substance abuse and our every move is dictated by our fleshly cravings for alcohol, cigarettes, crack, marijuana, or perverted sex.
10. Don't you get sick and tired of being sick and tired? Haven't you been broke, busted and disgusted long enough? Are you ready to stop banging your head against a wall that won't move?

VI. I'm coming out of the cave. I'm embracing my resurrection. I'm not going to give the enemy the satisfaction of my fear. I'm going to trust in Jesus and remember His promise, "Lo I am with you always even to the end of the world."

1. I don't know about you but I've been held back by traditionalism.
2. I'm tired of being oppressed by racism, discrimination, classism and gender bias.
3. I've been held down from advancement on my job too long.

4. I've compromised with people who had nothing to bargain with too often.
5. I've been detained against my will too long.
6. I've sat on my testimony too long.
7. I've almost bit a hole in my lip trying to keep from shouting.
8. I've been restrained from dancing in the aisle too long.
9. I'm through listening to critics and the doubters trying to tell me how to run my life and block me from my blessing. The devil is a liar! Don't you know I've got work to do! I can't let the world hold me back!
10. I've got higher places to go and important people to see.
11. I've got mountains to climb and rivers to cross, a praise to raise and victories to claim.
12. I've got a charge to keep and a God to glorify. I stopped by to tell you, *I Feel Like Bustin' Loose!*

CONCLUSION – In this story we read the shortest verse in the Bible. John writes, "Jesus wept." It's the shortest verse but it's loaded with meaning and wonder. Why would Jesus weep if He was about to do something miraculous that would transform everyone's tears into joy? Why shed tears when Martha and Mary would have their beloved brother with them again?

When Lazarus died his soul separated from his body and went home to be with the Lord. When he arrived in heaven the Father greeted him with a welcome kiss as a son returned home from a long journey. The angels in heaven outfitted him with a beautiful white robe, gold slippers, a gold ring and a crown of life. Everything fit perfectly. Then he was led to his space around the throne. A powerful angel told Lazarus to watch and worship. He looked up and saw heavenly creatures, cherubim and seraphim flying all over heaven. The creatures had six wings. He looked up and the twenty-four elders threw down their crowns before the throne. Four living beings covered with eyes were sayings, "Holy, Holy, Holy, Lord God Almighty, which was, and is, and is to come." Lazarus threw down his crown too and shouted, "Holy, Holy, Holy!" As he lay prostrate before He who sat on the great white throne he felt a tap on his shoulder. He turned to see who it was and there stood the strong angel again. He said, "Lazarus I hate to disturb you but you've got a call in the office." Lazarus said, "Are you sure it's for me, I just got here?" The angel said, "The Master is come and calleth for thee. Lazarus asked the angel, "What about my spot?" the angel replied, "Don't worry the Son has prepared a place for you. When you return, you can pick up where you left off." Lazarus went to the front office. When He picked up the phone he heard the Lord calling and he immediately returned to his body, healed and disease free. Bond and gagged he somehow managed to emerge from the grave. Jesus wept because he had to recall his beloved friend from reward back to labor.

Two weeks later, Jesus Himself would repeat this resurrection motif when He died one Friday afternoon. After watching Him bleed to death, Joseph and Nicademus claimed His battered body, wrapped Him in linen cloth and laid Him in a borrowed grave. He lay there bound by the sins of the world for three days. But early on Sunday morning He got up and *bust loose* from death, hell and the grave, holding all power in His hands. He *bust loose* and took captivity captive. He *bust loose* and now hell can't hold me. He *bust loose* and now the grave can't keep me. He *bust loose* and now death is defeated!

~ November 26, 2006

CHAPTER 3
PRAISE

The Theory of Praise	98
The King of the Jungle	102
Fight the Power	105
From Tragedy to Triumph	110
It's Electric	118
Another Night With the Frogs	132
I Can't Hold My Peace	146
The Expedient Route	156

The Theory of Praise

One of the elementary truths of physics is Sir Isaac Newton's Law of gravitation which simply states; "The force of attraction between any two masses in the universe is directly proportional to the product of the masses and inversely proportional to the square of the distance between their centers of mass" or $E=MC^2$.

This scientific equation is parallel to an elementary truth of faith, something I like to call the law of spiritual gravity. Simply put it declares: When praises go up, blessings come down or $B=P^2$.

It is not my intent to be facetious though the concept is quaint. Spiritual gravity... In essence earthly praises to God causes heavenly blessings to fall from God. That sounds like the law of Divine relativity. *(That's another article)*.

It seems that God gets quite a kick out of praise. The longest book of the bible, Psalms *(Praises)*, is dedicated to just that. In the psalms King David declared, "I will bless the Lord at all times: His praise shall continually be in my mouth" (Psalms 34:1). Obviously praise is not a part time job we only employ when things are going our way.

THE THEORY OF PRAISE

Praise is the mortal response to God's supernatural revelation of Himself. From the Latin tongue praise means, *"value"*, or *price"*. In our praise of God we express His value and worth to us. A songwriter has declared, "From the rising of the sun until the going down of the same, Jesus, blessed Savior, is worthy to be praised."

There are multitudes of ways to render praise unto God. You can sing… "Sing praises to the Lord, which dwelleth in Zion: declare among the people His doing" (Psa. 9:11). If you can't carry a note, why not try dancing? That's what Moses big sister Miriam did when God parted the Red Sea and Israel crossed on dry land (Exodus 15:20). So did David when the Ark of the Lord was brought into Jerusalem (2 Sam 6:14) (Please try to keep your clothes on). How about with instruments? Psalms 150 instructs us to praise God with trumpets, psaltery, harp, timbrel, stringed instruments, organs, loud cymbals and high sounding cymbals. In fact everything that has breath (the whole band) is to praise the Lord! Maybe you can shout? That's what Joshua told the children of Israel to do and the walls of Jericho fell (Joshua 6:20).

Praise seems to have a bi-polar effect. Through praise God is glorified, man is edified and Satan is horrified. Peter observed this when he wrote to the early church: "But ye are a chosen generation a royal priest hood, an holy nation, a peculiar people; that ye should shew forth the praises of him who hath called you out of darkness into his marvelous light (Peter 2:9). Praise is our invitation to God. It is our gift to Him. God actually enjoys our praise and He inhabits it!

You know, He kind of pulls up a seat and inclines His holy ear. Because of your praise God is moved to bless you. To "barak" you. To expand your territory and to show divine favor upon your life. To add your increase. To elevate you from faith to faith and from glory to glory. When you find yourself in the midst of a storm in life and still the fruit of your lips is the sacrifice of praise, the law of spiritual gravity goes into effect. A fellow by the name of Job will attest to that. He will tell you that your blessing is on the other side of whatever you are going through. Job lost all he had to the point of serious illness. On his bed of affliction he told three concerned friends, "Though He slay me, yet will I trust Him... All the days of my appointed time will I wait till my change come." Before it was all over God restored Job two times that which he previously lost. That's double for your trouble! (That's another article) Hallelujah!

~ March 16, 2005

The King of the Jungle

On a field trip to the North Carolina Zoological Park in Asheboro, the children enrolled in our Summer Youth Workshop were in total awe of the many exotic animals from all over the world. They saw beautiful birds of all colors and sizes. They saw reptiles like snakes, lizards, turtles, and crocodiles. They marveled at the giant African elephants, zebras, rhinoceros, and cheetah. They saw Bengal tigers of Asia, camels from India, and grizzly bears from North America.

Then we passed the lion exhibit and they were amazed at the size and strength of the king of beasts. It was at this impasse that a six year-old named Nijhi asked a poignant question. He wanted to know, "Which animal is strongest?"

I flinched! A thought hit me. The strongest beast of all is not in the zoo or in the jungle. The world's strongest and most dangerous beast is that pink thing in our mouths, commonly known as the tongue.

The tongue is a phenomenal creature. It houses our sense of taste and affects our sense of smell. The Old Testament stressed the practical results of the use of the tongue for the individual's life (Prov. 12:18; 18:21; 25:23 and 28:23). In the New Testament James likened the tongue to a bit in a horse's mouth or rudder of a ship, in that the tongue could control the direction of a person's life (James 3:1-8).

The tongue can do fascinating things. It can praise the Lord. The tongue can exalt the name of the most high God. The tongue can complement and congratulate. The tongue can sing songs that soothe our hearts. The tongue has been heard to say, "I love you, 'May I' and 'thank you'." <u>While the tongue can do so many wonderful things, it has been known to be destructive.</u>

On one occasion, the Pharisees challenged Jesus for not ceremoniously washing His hands before dinner. His reply to them was, "It's not what we digest that defiles us. It's what we say that blemishes us."

In his great wisdom, man has tamed and trained many ferocious beasts. The circus is full of wild animals under the control of the ringmaster. The aquarium is overflowing with tamed sea creatures. One wild animal has eluded the nets of seamen and traps of hunters...the tongue. The same tongue that praises the Lord can curse God's greatest creation. The same tongue that compliments also criticizes. The same tongue that congratulates also condemns. The tongue that sings, also slanders. The tongue that speaks of love and appreciation, also breathes lies and gossip... And you thought the lion was king...

~ June 16, 2001

Fight The Power!

I was in a deep sleep-dreaming. I was in a high pulpit. An old lady had almost fallen over the ledge. Fortunately, I caught her before she fell to her death. As I signaled for help, two old chairs were moved. I fell forward with the women and landed safely.

After this, the great pulpit was set up in five sections before a vast audience. There was a double seat in the middle with a small refreshment table beside it. There were two side chairs. A chair in the rear right and near the front edge left an area of two or three seats where I think someone was sitting. There was a row of seats on the right wall where only men sat, as well as, a row on the left where only women sat.

The stage was set. Everyone was dressed casual. I was, seemingly, in my PJs. The lights were dimmed. I began to narrate in the background, telling the crowd about the many trials that I knew they had been through. I wanted them to forget those things that were in the painful past. As I was encouraging the multitude, a man on my right shouted something to a woman on my left. It seems humorous at first, but then the woman responded with a remark that infuriated the man. He shouted back at the woman, who was now walking over to him. I attempted to calm the situation, but no one could hear me, or maybe they just ignored me. Finally, I came down out of the pulpit and told them they had to leave with their argument. She invited him outside and they left the building.

By this time, I'm at the rear of the church adjusting my clothes. My ragged socks are but hanging off. I tell the remaining crowd that we had just been attacked by the devil. That he had just attempted to disrupt our praise and worship of God by causing a chaotic situation in this morning service.

I explained to the people how he once was a beautiful angel named Lucifer and how he was the reflection of or mirror image of the Lord. I showed them how he went everywhere that God went reflecting the Lord's beauty. I told them that one day Satan became jealous or he began to lust for some of the praise that God received. He organized a mutiny that failed and so God swiftly and decisively kicked Lucifer out of Heaven and erased his name from the honor rolls of

Heaven and gave him an ugly name, Satan (the adversary), the enemy of God. Right here, I began to transition from sleep to semi-consciousness. The enemy does not want me to finish the dream. He interrupted the dream with a distraction. Now he wants to wake me up before I can rebuke him.

As I begin to wake, I'm still somehow dreaming. I tell the audience, "I rebuke Satan and all his demons to the very pits of hell from whence they came, in the name of Jesus! I call him out as a liar and a murderer from the beginning. Now he's really trying to wake me up because the people are feeling the vibe that God gave me. They can sense the anointing as I adjust my clothing I'm experiencing cold chills as I write. Then I quote Luke 10:18 where our Savior told the disciples, "I beheld Satan as lightning fell from Heaven". The whole house shook when I told them what Jesus said. I feel great joy and a sense of wholeness.

The dream was over. My eyes were opened. I was walking to the refrigerator to grab something to drink. I felt tired. The way I sometimes feel after preaching hard. I realized then, that God was sending me a message in my sleep. The devil slipped in his own message while God was transmitting to my mind.

Many times Satan has foiled messages intended to minister to me. He bit off more than he could chew this time. God used Satan's message to send me a greater message, a powerful revelation. He showed me that what the enemy meant for evil, God meant it for good, to bring it to pass, to save me alive. God showed me that I still have a work to do in His church. Despite the enemy's attacks, I must stick to my assignment and lay waste to the enemy.

I'm experiencing great chills now. The Spirit is using me at 6:31 a.m. I've got a word to give to the people of God. The title is from a movie theme. A song made popular by the rap group Public Enemy…Fight the Power! Paul writes in Romans 8, "Nothing, not even powers shall be able to separate us from the love of God". In Ephesians 6, he reminds us that we are not fighting people or personalities, but our fight is against principalities, powers the devil and his evil plots to destroy God's greatest creation.

With a new zeal and commitment, I vow to, "Fight the Powers that be". Fight the Power! With every fiber of my being, I must fight the good fight of faith and lay claim to eternal life. I must not let fear of failure grip me. I will not quit. I will not turn around or look backward. I must never forget that Satan is a defeated foe. His army is headed for a destruction, like Pharaoh's (another devil) army in the Red Sea. Bring on the enemy. Bring on the next fool to fight. Have you not heard…The battle is not mine, it is the Lord's. Get pumped up. Even the storm clouds rise and war lurks in the balance, "We are more than conquerors through Him that loved us".

Victory is mine, victory is mine. Victory today is mine. I told Satan get thee behind. Victory today is mine!

~ October 1, 2002

From Tragedy to Triumph

In June 1993, the Lord guided me in the planting of New Covenant Missionary Baptist Church in Rock Hill, South Carolina. The little church grew quickly. Ministries flourished. One of the largest families in the new congregation was the Anthony's. In total, there were 29 of them. There was the mother Rachael, five daughters, their 13 children and their 10 children. When they all showed up at the same time, the little church would be rocking.

My oldest son Marquis was best friends with one of the Anthony grandchildren, Tyrone. During the summer they were inseparable. They spent the night at each other's house and matured into young men.

In June 1997, I was called to New Bethlehem Baptist Church in Philadelphia, PA. We left the little church that had grown to over 150 members and headed to the big city. Marquis graduated from High School. Tyrone finished the 11th grade. The two seemed to have different interest. Marquis had his eyes on North Carolina Central University, Durham, NC where he would become a percussionist in the marching band. Tyrone got caught up in the local drug culture. He was selling weed and often smoking the profits.

This was dragging him deeper into the hole with the local king pin. That August before I sent Marquis to Durham, I told him to check on Tyrone and encourage him to get back in church. Marquis reported that he had spoken with Tyrone's mother. She told him that Tyrone dropped out of school. He would leave home for weeks at a time. She said sometimes "thugs" would come to her house looking for Tyrone.

They were angry because he had borrowed money or sold product and then disappeared. Patricia had given up on Tyrone. I called her and prayed for Tyrone to be delivered from this drug demon that was crippling his life and destroying his future. She promised to keep me informed of Tyrone's progress. She loved her only son and did not want to lose him to the streets.

Three months later I got a phone call around 2:30 in the morning. The caller ID said Rock Hill, SC. I answered the phone. It was Marlon one of the Anthony grandchildren. He was sobbing. I sat up in the bed. I asked, "What's wrong Marlon?" He blurted out, "Pastor Tyrone is dead. Somebody killed him." I was stunned. I asked what happened. He wasn't sure, but he knew it had to do with drugs. I told Marlon to call me back when he had more details. The next morning I called Marquis and told him his best friend was dead. He took it hard. He dropped the phone and ran down the hallway of his dorm. I explained what happened to his roommate who found Marquis and consoled him.

Tyrone's aunt, one of my first members at New Covenant, called me two days later with details of Tyrone's murder. It was around 10 p.m. on a Friday night. Tyrone and two of his accomplices went to the home of a young man who was well known for moving large quantities of weed. One of the guys distracted him while Tyrone and another kid stole a couple of pounds of weed and ran. The guy realized he had been duped, grabbed his gun and chased the trio into the woods. He cornered them attempting to drive off. He called two of his partners who quickly came out to the scene. They lined the three thieves behind the car and shot them to death. They piled the corpses in the trunk and drove the car to a wooded are in another county. Then they set the car on fire to cover up the evidence.

The brutal killing was first thought to be the work of the Jamaicans who sold a lot of drugs in South Carolina. The police were somehow able to connect the killings to a teenaged drug dealer. There was suddenly a lot of racial tension in Rock Hill because the victims were all black and the perpetrators were all white. Six months later the victims' mothers and the perpetrators' parents appeared on an episode of "Montel".

A week later, I was back in Rock Hill, South Carolina. The family wanted me to preach Tyrone's funeral. I led Tyrone to Christ when he was 11. I baptized him. During the summer he all but lived at my house. I knew Tyrone so I agreed to eulogize him. The little church I planted in the community was too small to hold the service. I called Pastor Steve Hogg of First Baptist and asked if the family could use their facilities. He was very gracious. He thought this gesture might ease some of the tension in the city since his congregation was all white. I agreed.

The sanctuary at First Baptist could seat 800. They had to bring an additional 100 folding chairs. Even then there were people in the narthex and standing along the walls. Over a thousand were on hand to say good-bye to Tyrone.

I do not remember being sad when I arrived. I was calm and focused. After 200 plus funerals, it just seemed like another day at the office. My father always instructed me to avoid joining in "their" grief. He told me to never let them see you sweat! Of course the funeral directors did not open the casket so that took some of the edge off the crowd. His senior picture sat atop the bier.

The services started with the high school gospel choir singing. I was alone in the pulpit, no help that day, just me and God. I read the Old and New Testaments, and then led the congregation in a prayer of consolation. I wanted to move as succinct as possible to keep the congregation calm and spare the family more tears. Friends and family made remarks. These words seemed to lighten the mood. Cards and the obituary were read aloud by the church clerk from New Covenant. Then the choir sang again. This time the song had a victorious tone.

"Why should I feel discouraged? Why should the shadows come? Why should my heart be lonely and long for heaven and home? When Jesus is my portion; a constant friend is he. His eye is on the sparrow and I

know he watches me. I sing because I'm happy, I sing because I'm free. His eye is on the sparrow and I know He watches me."[14]

Amid a chorus of "Hallelujah', "Amen" and "Thank you Jesus", I approached the holy desk. I was ready to preach like never before. I could feel the hair stand on the back of my neck. After a few words of condolences and fond memories of the deceased, I took my text; Hebrews 9:27, "And as it is appointed unto men once to die, but after this the judgment". My sermon was entitled, *"The Unbreakable Appointment."* I started slow, the audience was quiet. As I gained momentum, I felt a peace and then a power surge come over me that made every word flow out of my mouth like water. I began to feel the authority to demand that these young people prepare for the day of reckoning. As I closed, the church was on fire. People were standing all over the building crying and waiving their hands. It was tragedy, but it sparked a revival. I returned to my seat content that I had truly communed with God.

The funeral directors came down the aisles to claim the remains and lead the family out of the church. Just then the

---

[14] Gabriel, Charles H. and Martin, Civilla D., *"His Eye is On the Sparrow"*, 1905

Holy Spirit spoke to me and I jumped to my feet. I told the audience, "If you want to see Jesus, if you want to live an abundant life, if you want to be saved from hell, you must make an appointment with Jesus right now. Come to Jesus before it is everlasting too late". I told the students if Tyrone could speak to you from heaven right now he would say, "Friends you must be born again." At that moment young people came from all over the building and filled the altar. It was so full I invited many into the pulpit with me. Many of them were weeping and others were sobbing uncontrollably. Some were accompanied by their parents.

The ushers lost count of the kids after 200. I told the young people to join hands and repeat after me. They joined hands and I led them in admitting that they were sinners, professing faith in Jesus as their risen Savior and committing their lives to following Him. When the prayer ended there was loud clapping. Shouts of praise and thanksgiving echoed all over the building. Parents were hugging their children and telling them they loved them.

My son came to me, put his arms around my shoulders and said, "Thanks Dad, Tyrone would have wanted it this way."

I thank God for that one opportunity he gave me to win so many souls for his glory at one time. It was my greatest worship experience. Like Joseph told his brothers in Egypt, "What the enemy meant for evil, the Lord meant it if for good, to bring it to pass, to save much people alive" (Gen 50:20).

~ June, 2008

It's Electric!
Acts 17:28

TEXT - *For in him we live, and move, and have our being; as certain of your own poets have said, For we are also His offspring.*

EXPOSITION - Our text finds Paul on his second Missionary journey around 52 AD. He and Barnabas the Encourager had earlier parted ways because the latter insisted on taking his nephew John Mark with them. Earlier Mark had deserted the group at Pamphylia and returned to Jerusalem. Now Paul had no confidence in Mark's commitment to the mission. Paul chose Silas for the second tour and headed to Greece. Adding Timothy to the caravan in Lystra, they revisited the cities of Galatia. In Troas or ancient Troy, the evangelist Luke joined the party and traveled with them to Philippi at the northeastern corner of Greece. This was the setting for the first European church planted by Paul, followed by Thessalonica, 100 miles west. Chased out of town by lewd fellows of the baser sort or thugs to be succinct, the group fled Thessalonica for Berea.

The spiteful Jews found out their work in Berea and followed them there, again creating trouble and causing the brethren to quickly sneak Paul out of town. They shipped the Apostle down to Athens an influential port city at the Southern tip of Greece for refuge.

Athens, named for Athenia the Greek goddess of wisdom, was the Greek center of art, philosophy, literature, science, commerce, and the home of one of the world's most renowned universities. It was also the birthplace of such philosophers as Pericles, Socrates, Demosthenes and Plato. The Athenians were idol worshipper's renowned for erecting altars to every god imaginable; not in adoration or worship, but in fear or caution.

Troubled in his spirit by this atmosphere of vain worship the Apostle took his gospel message to the local synagogue, the market place and the streets. Word spread through the city that there was a new guy in town teaching a strange new philosophy about a man named Jesus of Nazareth, who though crucified, had redeemed humanity from sins. He been raised from the dead and now ascended to the right hand of God.

So the philosophers summoned Paul to a public assembly at Areopagus or Mars Hill to hear this revolutionary doctrine. The Apostle reprimanded them for their worship of the unknown god, whom they reverenced ignorantly. For this reason Paul summarized that they were too superstitious.

They were so careful to try and honor every deity that they went so far as to erect an altar to the unknown god just in case. Paul told them that this God whom they acknowledged ignorantly, he knew through a personal encounter on a Damascus highway. He declared to them the mighty work of God in creation (Elohim). He explained that God was not confined or limited by manmade devices, but that He alone is indeed the maker of everything in the earth.

EXEGESIS - Paul explained to them that our God is the Father of the entire universe. He is Elohim the creator and sustainer of all that is, was and ever will be. No tent or temple could ever contain Him. No shrine could ever capture His omniscience. No man-made building is suitable for His habitation. No pavilion could ever encompass Him. There is nothing we can do to increase or decrease Him. He alone is omnipotent. He alone gives life.

God said, I, even I, am the Lord, and apart from me there is no savior. I have revealed, saved, and proclaimed and I, am not some foreign god among you. You are my witnesses, declares the Lord, that I am God (Is 43:11-13). He made us all of one blood. We all evolve from one common creation event.

INTRODUCTION - Reggae Superstar Marcia Griffiths recorded a R&B song in the 1980's that ignited a line dance craze still popular today affectionately called the "Electric Boogie".[15] Ironically, the song has theological implications when paralleled with the content of our text. I'm sure you are familiar with these catchy lyrics, "Some say it's a mystic, its electric boogie woogie … woogie! You can't do without it, its electric boogie woogie … woogie! You can't see it, its electric boogie woogie … woogie! You've got to feel it, its electric boogie woogie … woogie! But you know it's there … here, there, and everywhere.

---

[15] Griffiths, Marcia, "*Electric Boogie*", Mango/Island Records, 1989

TEARS OF A CLOWN

I. The first lyric of the song that grabs our attention is the observation that some say "it's a mystic."

1. The philosophers on Mars Hill were guilty of attributing the mighty works of God to some mystical, imaginary deity. They were so careful to acknowledge every god known to the Greeks that they heaped the Maker and Sustainer of the Universe on the same pile as their little demigods.

2. We are often guilty of saying, "It's a mystic". Many things happen in our lives that we classify as "good luck, bad luck or coincidence." We attribute many of our experiences to "fate or happen chance." How many times have I heard someone throwing dice say "Come on Lady Luck," and then crap out.

3. We've seen people with a lucky rabbit's foot on their key chain (I imagine the rabbit didn't feel so lucky). What about the horse shoe over the door, that's a lucky charm until it falls off the nail and bust somebody's head. How about the salt over the shoulder trick? That will keep the evil spirits away. Don't forget to wish on a falling star and pluck a four leaf clover.

4. As a child I was told: Don't step on a crack in the sidewalk you'll break your momma's back. Don't split the pole (that could be deadly). If a black cat cross your path, turn around and go another way. And whatever you do don't waste your wish bone, wishing on something stupid.

5. In many instances we are just too superstitious for our own good. Superstition leads to paranoia and paranoia leads to obsession. That's why King Saul disguised himself and went to visit the witch of Endor late one night. He tricked her into conjuring up the spirit of the late prophet Samuel who informed him that he would die on the battlefield the next day (maybe he should have quit while he was ahead).

6. Believing in mystics makes us buy lottery tickets with our last dollar. The mystics make us want to call Ms. Cleo on the psychic hot line and tell her all our problems. The mystics make us go on online and check our horoscope every day. The mystics make us spread goober dust around our house. The mystics have us shaking a bag of chicken bones up

and pouring them out on the table to predict the future.

7. The problem we as Christians should have with mystics or the occult or the superstitious is we know that there is no luck in God. There is no coincidence in Christ. You cannot surprise the King of Glory. He that watches Israel neither sleeps nor slumbers. Every good and perfect gift comes from God who needs no tricks to bless your soul. And what God has for me, it is for me.

II. Then the song writer said, "You can't do without it".

1. Many people have learned the hard way that you can't do without God. David declared, "If it had not been for the Lord on my side my soul would have dwelt in silence."

2. It is folly to believe that we can at any moment escape from the all seeing eye of God. He knows our every step. He knows every beat of our hearts, every thought of our brains.

3. He has ordered our steps and even numbered the hairs upon our heads.

4. Even the unbeliever and the unrepentant continue to exist if only by God's abundant grace and mercy.

IT'S ELECTRIC!

       Matthew 5:45 says, "He maketh His sun to rise on the evil and on the good, and sendeth rain on the just and the unjust.

5. Even those who make it big and live the life of the rich and famous, blinging, highballing, and shot calling cannot make it without God.
6. In Luke 12, Jesus told us the parable of the rich farmer who laid up great treasure for himself in barns and storehouses. The same night he bragged about how much he had, God called him "fool" and told him "This night thy soul shall be required of thee: then whose shall these things be?"
7. We need Him for our everyday substance. That's why Jesus taught us to pray, "Give us this day our daily bread."
8. We worship Him and call His name Jehovah Jireh, our provider. No wonder the doxology sings, "All things come of thee O Lord and of thine own, have we given thee."

III. Then Ms. Griffiths tells us … "You can't see it."
    1. When Israel came out of Egypt after more than 400 years, they had some excess baggage.

They had been exposed to Pharaoh and Egyptian polytheism. They had become familiar with the worship of statues and graven images. After crossing the Red Sea on dry land and seeing God vanish their enemies, they built themselves a golden calf and fired God. They wanted a god they could see, touch and manipulate.

2. You can't see God with the natural eye because "God is a spirit" and they that worship Him must worship Him in spirit and truth (John 4:24).

3. Your naked eye cannot behold such glory. Our minds cannot comprehend that much truth. Your heart cannot hold that much compassion. We cannot look upon that level of holiness.

4. No wonder God told Moses, "Thou canst not see my face; for there shall no man see me and live."

5. Elijah, the great prophet from Tishbe stood on the mountain before the Lord waiting to see Him. A mighty gust of wind tore the mountain apart. A powerful earthquake shook the mountain to its foundation. Later fire engulfed the fortress. God was neither in the wind, the earthquake nor the fire but in a small still voice. No you can't see God. But that doesn't diminish who He is.

IV. The lyricist challenges our spiritual relationship with God when he says, "You've got to feel it."
   1. Many people go to church every Sunday like they are going to work on Monday. Tired, dragging, irritable and disconnected. Church has become little more than ritual and routine. They leave feeling just as empty and despondent as they did when they came in door.
   2. They can't feel anything because they walk in the door with a defeated attitude and a loser mentality.
   3. Your plate is so full of junk you can't get to your break through. Your personal issues are blocking your blessings. It's hard to feel it when your heart is numb from the bumps and bruises of trying to make a dollar out of 15 cents.
   4. Yet, we must press our way to the alter and lay prostrate before the Lord and cry out to the God of our Salvation until we feel the spirit move.
   5. That's the way King David admonished us to, "Enter into His gates with thanksgiving and into His courts with praise: be thankful unto Him and bless His name (Psalm 100:4)."

6. Jeremiah felt it. He wanted to quit preaching. He tried to keep quiet in the synagogue. But the word of God was too much for the prophet to maintain. He said the word of God was in his heart and it felt like fire shut up in his bones (Jer 20:9).
7. David "felt it", when the Ark of the Covenant was returned to Jerusalem. The spirit of God fell on David so strong he danced out his robe and "partied like a rock star, totally dude."
8. When you feel it you run though nobody's chasing you. You laugh though nobody told a joke. You might even cry though nobody's sad. You start waving your hands or stomping your feet or speaking in unknown tongues because you feel it deep down in your soul.

V. What makes this dance hit so theologically and biblically sound is the punch line or the hook of the song. Marcia says, "But you know it's there … here … there and everywhere."

1. The lyricist makes me want to dance. Not because the beat is so good, but because my God is so good to me. You can't see the electricity illuminating this building, but you know it's there. You can't see the music

coming out the organ, but you know it's there. You can't see the wind blow, yet when the trees sway from side to side, you see its effect. She's saying that God is omnipresent. One songwriter said, "He's everywhere I go, everywhere I be. Not only that, He's the same yesterday, today, and forever".

2. You see, God is a circle whose center is everywhere and whose circumference is nowhere, so the seamless circle is the symbol of His endless love for His creation.

3. The sweet psalmist of Israel asked, "Whither shall I go from thy spirit or whither shall I flee from thy presence?"

4. It's good to know God is on my left and on my right; in front and behind, over me and under me and He's keeping me alive.

5. It gives me joy when I realize that the God I serve is Jehovah – Shamma. The Lord is There and He's right on time.

CONCLUSION - I just want you to think about the spiritual overtones and theological contours of the song "Electric Boogie" the next time someone drags you out on the dance floor at a birthday party, wedding reception or family reunion. then you hear Marcia Griffiths say, "It's Electric", you'll turn the party out if you throw up your hands and shout "Hallelujah". For surely everything in the universe is electric. The wind, rain, sun, moon, plants and animals, rivers and streams, the earth rotating 360 degrees on its axis every day, it's all electric. God's Shekinah glory is like a super-atomic current of energy, giving vitality to the entire universe. He empowers, encourages, enhances, enlightens, enriches and electrifies the galaxy. Not only did God electrify the universe, but He put His power in mankind.

God breathed into man's nostrils and he became a living soul. The Ruach Hakodesh (Mighty Wind) of God was like a sudden jolt of dunamis running through our veins. Man became animated. Man developed character and creative capability. But man sinned against God in the Garden of Eden and his power bill came due. Man was given extensions time and time again while the bill gained late charges and penalties. God looked through heaven for somebody to go to earth and rectify humanities debt before Satan cut off our power. Noah couldn't go, he got drunk and got his lights cut off one time. Abraham couldn't go he lied and his lights were disconnected. Moses couldn't go, he killed somebody and ended up sitting in the dark. David couldn't go, he stole a man's wife and got a disconnection notice. Solomon couldn't go. All those wives and concubines ran his bill sky high. But Jesus stepped up with a perfect credit report. He paid paid the late penalties, deposits and back charges for 42 generations. He suffered and died on an old rugged cross to redeem a lost world. Old man death cut off His power on Friday evening. Grave closed His account on Saturday. But early on Sunday morning, God bought the company and quickly electrified Jesus who rose from the dead with all power in His hands.

The devil is a lie, it's not mystic! It's electric! I can't do without it because it's electric. No, you can't see it, but you can't make me doubt it, because I know too much about it. OOOOOO shocking! Aren't you glad that you know it's there? Here, there, and everywhere!

~ August 5, 2007

Another Night With the Frogs
Exodus 8:9-10

TEXT - *And Moses said unto Pharaoh, Glory over me: When shall I intreat for thee, and for thy servants, and for thy people, to destroy the frogs from thee and thy houses, that they may remain in the river only? And he said,* **tomorrow***. And he said, be it according to thy word: that thou mayest know that there is none like unto the Lord our God.*

EXPOSITION - Our text today is taken from the 2nd book of the Torah during the early 19th dynasty of Egypt around 1490BC. The book of Exodus (the 2nd book of Moses) is a treasure chest of early Hebrew history. In Exodus sides are clearly drawn. On the one side we see Pharaoh Thotmas whose kingdom was prospering on the backs of Hebrew slaves. On the other hand we see Elohim Almighty God being represented by Moses and his younger brother the high priest, Aaron as spokesman. The great conflict is defined in simple terms. God demanded freedom for the children of Israel, that they might secure the promised land which He had given them in the wilderness. Pharaoh wanted to keep Israel enslaved for Egyptian economic stability and political clout in the African Delta region. At the center of this great conflict was Moses, God's delivery boy, the interpreter of Gods works, the mediator of the covenant. Moses was sent back to Egypt by God to demand that Pharaoh, "Let My People Go". When Pharaoh would not heed to the demand of God, the Lord made Egypt to suffer ten painful plagues, breaking the oppressors spirit and freeing God's people. The second plague on Egypt is our focal point today. The plague of the frogs...

I. Let us note today that Pharaoh brought the plagues on himself. He had been repeatedly and duly warned by Moses that if he refused to let God's people go Egypt would suffer.
   1. God had already turned the majestic River Nile into blood causing great discomfort and unrest in Egypt. Man nor beast could find anything cool to wet their parched tongues. The bloody river caused all the fish to die and float to the surface of the river and the odor in Egypt was very foul. Time and time again Pharaoh was warned but he did not heed.
   2. After seven days of bloody river God turned the Nile back into water. Pharaoh figured that the worst was

over, that he had somehow with- stood what he thought was God's best trick.

3. But, Moses returned a second time and told Pharaoh, the Lord told me to tell you let my people go that they may serve me, or else I will attack you with frogs!

4. Pharaoh thought; "Moses your God is very comical. Attack the majesty of the great Osiris and Isis with frogs? Not with great men of war in 10,000 armored chariots. Not with lions or bears or mighty tigers. Not with hyena or wolves or the giant elephant, but with the slimy little frog. Yeah right. Go ahead and send your frogs Moses. Tell your God to send His amphibious soldiers, but I shall never let Israel go."

5. Yes, Pharaoh had <u>been warned</u>. He knew the consequences of His actions, yet he chose to ignore God's command. He did not take God seriously. He thought the invisible God of the Hebrews to be mere superstition or folklore.

6. Because Pharaoh disobeyed God, Aaron was instructed to stretch forth his hands over all the bodies of water in Egypt and cause frogs to come out of the water and upon the land of Egypt.

7. When Aaron summoned the frogs for the Lord, frogs came from everywhere and got into everything. Frogs were in the palace. Frogs were in the temple. Frogs were in the kitchen. Frogs in the toilet. Frogs in the court house. Frogs in the bedroom. Frogs in the chariots. Frogs in the closet. Frogs in the food. Frogs in folks clothes. All over the living room floor. In the bath tub. In Pharaohs wine glass. All over the supper table. Everywhere you turned there were those nasty little, once insignificant, now unbearable…frogs!

8. Look at Pharaoh now. Perplexed. Upset. Disgruntled. He decided to take matters into his own hands. He was going to make the God of Moses acknowledge the sovereignty of Pharaoh. He called his magicians, soothsayers, fortune tellers and palm readers together and told them

to show the God of Israel that we can make frogs too. So the magicians cast their spells and potions over the waters as Pharaoh ordered them to do. And sure enough frogs came forth upon the land, just like God brought them upon the land. But what Pharaoh failed to realize was that the real trick wasn't making more frogs, the trick was getting rid of the frogs.

9. The magicians only made matters worse. Now the frogs doubled. Everywhere you stepped there were frogs. Everywhere you sat, there were frogs. Everywhere you looked there were frogs. Close your eyes and you could hear them ... rebit ... rebit ... close your ears and you could smell them, Oh the stench! Pharaoh could not even lay down on his couch, frogs would lay down with him. He had frogs and couldn't get rid of them.

   II. So finally Pharaoh gave up. He saw that he was licked or croaked (if you would). Pharaoh called Moses and Aaron back to the palace. He told them; In treat (petition, ask or pray) the Lord (not your Lord, not Israel's Lord not the Jews Lord, not the Hebrews Lord, but The Lord Elshaddi) that He may take away the frogs from me and from my people; and I will let the people go, that they may do sacrifice unto the Lord.

1. But notice in verse 2 when Moses asked Pharaoh; when shall I pray to the Lord to take away the frogs from you and your people and your homes and your beds and all about you and destroy them, that they remain only in the river, the reply that Pharaoh gave. The great king said, *tomorrow*.
2. Isn't that odd? Isn't that peculiar? Don't you find that idiosyncratic that Pharaoh didn't jump at the chance to get rid of the frogs right away?
3. You would think that Pharaoh would had said, do it now! It would seem logical that Pharaoh would have told Moses and Aaron take your frogs with you. Don't leave until you get rid of these frogs. Yet Pharaoh said *tomorrow*. Not now, not immediately, not momentarily but, *tomorrow*.

TRANSITION - Pharaoh was content to spend … Another Night with the Frogs.

Had Pharaoh grown fond of the little froggies and desired a few more precious moments to play with them? Had Pharaoh grown accustomed to their sing song in the night (rebit, rebit). What was it that made him say tomorrow?

1. The same things that made Pharaoh say tomorrow makes us say tomorrow. Pharaoh thought that if he waited until tomorrow he could possibly work things out himself. He thought that maybe he could get things in place by then. Maybe things would work themselves out by tomorrow? Maybe all the frogs would get sick and die before tomorrow? Maybe his magic men could come up with a potion to make the frogs disappear before the deadline and he would not owe any gratitude to God?

2. So many people are waiting on tomorrow. People in here right now are waiting till they get ready to make a change, hoping they can work things out themselves. Some of our family situations are all jacked up because we have failed to make the head of our family and home. Homes are wrecked. Why? Because we have not made God the head of our homes. We want to do it ourselves. We think we can do all the home

improvements on our own but, don't you know that "Except the Lord builds the house, they labor in vain that build it: except the Lord keep the city, the watchman waketh but in vain (Psalms 27:1)."

3. Like Pharaoh many people haven't turned to God yet because they want to get their life in order first. I hear it too often. I'm sick to my stomach of hearing seemingly rational people say; when I get my life in order I'm coming to church. I'm sick of hearing people say, when the time feels right I'll join.

4. I'm fed up with people who say, "I got to go home and pray about it! I'll be back next week" ... But if you die tonight sinner, you'll be standing outside. Wake up before it's too late. Paul declared, "The wages of sin is death, but the gift of God is eternal life" (Rom 6:23). People talking about I'm a member over yonder, but have not stepped foot in church in years. Backslider what are you waiting on? Oh, I forgot, tomorrow.

5. Like Pharaoh of the 19th dynasty of Egypt, the church is full of procrastinators. People who are willing to put off till tomorrow, what they can do today. Miss Lady, when are you going to take that dusty bible off the shelf and read it?... Tomorrow. Mr. Man when are you going to start attending church … Tomorrow. Miss Lady when are you going to start paying your tithes? … After I pay off some of these bills. Mr. Man when are you going to start attending Sunday School? I'm too tired. Mr. Man when are you going to be the leader you are supposed to be? … I've got to straighten some things out first … The Lord understands … He knows my heart … Yes God knows your heart, He understands. But God is no fool. "Be not dismayed, God is not mocked. What soever a man soweth that shall he reap".

6. How can you say you love the Lord and put the world before Him. How can you say you're living for Jesus and doing everything else you're big enough to do, contrary to His will? … We make time to go to the game, go to the movie, go to the mall, go to the party, go to the dance, go to the sorority or fraternity

or lodge meeting, but we get sick when someone asks us to go to bible study, Sunday School or morning worship, hypocrites!

7. We can find money for beer, lottery tickets, cigarettes, cable TV, extensions, Grecian formula, hair-cuts, weave-ins, fingernails and yard sales. But let someone ask us to sacrifice and pay our tithes and offerings and all of a sudden we develop a complex and start mumbling and grumbling under our breath. Its sick, the things we put in front of God. Someone ask you to sit on the board of trustees at Bank of America or Springs Foundation or one of the state commissions and you'll break your neck to be at all the meetings on time. Yet God blesses us with life, health and strength and the Pastor ask us to sing on the choir, usher or teach Sunday School or a volunteer tutor and we get mad, pitch a fit, start griping and making excuses. Don't you realize that to whom much is given, much is required? If you don't humble yourselves and obey God you'll be spending ... another night with the frogs.

III. It amazes me how people in and out of the church have an acquired Las Vegas mentality. They gamble with their lives, even their very souls. People live dangerously as if they control tomorrow. How often have I heard someone say "I'll take my chances and see what happens."
   1. They put their lives on the <u>roulette</u> table of life, living without the hope of salvation in Christ.
   2. They put their lives on the <u>blackjack</u> table of substance abuse hoping to avoid addiction by casual use.
   3. They put their lives in the <u>slot machine</u> of material wealth hoping to avoid a multitude of debt while living the glamorous life.
   4. They put their lives on the <u>crap table</u> of lies, hoping that they won't get caught in one. While trying to cover another one.
   5. We gamble with our lives thinking that tomorrow will come. We always have tomorrow don't we? I'll see what happens tomorrow. I don't know what tomorrow may bring, I only know who brings tomorrow.

6. Maybe some people lay their bets on tomorrow because they have grown accustomed to frogs. Some people have been living with frogs so long waiting on them to turn into prince charming that they don't even notice them anymore.

7. They've been living in their sins for so long that sin has become second nature. They've been doing wrong for so long that wrong seems right. Why stop now? If it feels right it must be right. If it feels good why stop? Remember you ain't hurting anybody (but yourself).

8. Maybe I'm just simple but I just can't see living with frogs. No matter how hard you try you can't change a frog into a good wife or a faithful husband. Why would you dare spend another night with pest in your bed? Why would you take a chance on being lost? Why would you put it off another day? Why would you risk leaving here today without being saved? Why would you trust the world and not God? Jehovah's voice is speaking to you even today, to come home right now and yet, we want to wait and see how things look tomorrow.

Don't you realize the longer you procrastinate the more blessings you forfeit? The longer you hesitate and vacillate the more suffering you endure.

TRANSITION - Don't spend another restless night with indecision. Surrender to Jesus while the blood runs warm in your veins.

CONCLUSION - I had a friend in junior high school who I was often in the company of. One Friday I spent the night at his house. Everywhere I went in the house there were roaches, in the bedroom, in the bathroom, in the TV room, everywhere. I didn't want to embarrass my friend so I didn't comment on their presence. When we went to bed that night I fell asleep and forgot about the bugs. But, in the middle of the night I woke up to find a parade of roaches crawling across my chest. I jumped out of bed screaming at the top of my lungs, "Get these roaches off me." My friend looked at me with little concern and said, "Man go back to sleep. The roaches live here too! They just going to the kitchen to get some leftovers."

I'm searching for a breakthrough. I'm not going to go another night with the frogs. You don't have to tolerate the frogs in your life another night. You can ask the Savior and right now, immediately, in a hurry, Jesus will rescue you. You don't have to take the chance of waiting till tomorrow and dying in your sins tonight. Now is our salvation closer than ever. Now God is doing a new thing. Behold I do a new thing saith, the Lord. Shall ye not see it. Shall it not spring forth? I will make a way in the wilderness and rivers in the desert," (Isaiah 43:19). Can't you see the wondrous love of Jesus? He died on Calvary so that you would not have to wait until tomorrow for redemption, you can have it right now! You don't have to take a test or perform any stunts. Only trust him. Only believe that Jesus Christ is the Son of God. Believe that he died on the Cross and that God raised Him from the dead on the 3rd day morning, you will be delivered immediately and not tomorrow!

~April 28, 2010

I Can't Hold My Peace
Luke 18: 39 (NIV)

Text: *And they which went before rebuked him, that he should hold his peace; but he cried so much the more, Thou son of David, have mercy on me.*

EXPOSITION - In the spring of 29 AD, Jesus on his way to Jerusalem approached the city of Jericho. Traveling on the Jericho road accompanied by a great multitude of followers, Jesus was the center of attention. Along the roadside were beggars and blind men, who were happy to hear the crowd buzzing in hopes that they would receive generous donations or alms from the throng. Included in this group of men and beggars was a certain blind man. Luke leaves him nameless, but Mark records his name to have been Bartimaeus, son of Timaeus.

When Bartimaeus heard the noise of the crowd he began to inquire and ask why was everyone so excited? What's happening? Where is everyone going? Someone told the blind man that Jesus of Nazareth was passing by on his way to Jerusalem. Bartimaeus recognized the name. Oh yes, Jesus. Isn't that Mary's oldest son? Isn't that the one John baptized at the River Jordan? Is that the one who turned water into wine at a wedding reception in Canaan of Galilee? Jesus. . . Is that the one who fed 5000 with two fish and five barley loaves? Jesus. . . Isn't he the one who raised Lazarus up from the dead? . . . Jesus. . . I heard he makes the lame walk, the deaf hear, and even restores sight to the blind!... Jesus. . . His divine reputation preceded him.

When Bartimaeus realized that the Great Physician was in close proximity, he began to shout and scream, "Jesus thou son of David, have mercy on me."
INTRODUCTION - Look at how God cares for us. Though Bartimaeus could not see with the natural eye, God sharpened his hearing so that he could distinctively hear voices, though they were distant. God turned up the volume of Bartimeaus' voice so that even in a mob everyone could hear him shout, "Jesus thou son of David, have mercy on me." When you think someone is handicapped in one capacity, God is over compensating them in another way. God is always making up for natures negligence. Because He is more than a doctor, God specializes.

When Bartimeaus began to shout at the top of his voice to the Master, those in the front (the leaders) began to rebuke Bartimaeus. They told the blind man to shut up, hush, be quiet, don't scream out Jesus' name like that. Their rebuke only made Bartimaeus scream louder, "Thou Son of David have mercy on me." He heard the blind man's cry. Jesus will hear our faintest cry. He stopped in his tracks and summoned the blind man to him. When he was brought near, Jesus asked him; " What do you want me to do for you?" Bartimaeus said: " Lord, I want to see." Jesus said, Receive your sight, your faith has healed you. And <u>immediately</u> the blind was no longer blind; he began to see and shout and praise God, and the great crowd saw the miracle and they too shouted and praised God for His loving kindness and tender mercies. When considering how the good Lord has delivered me and saved me and picked me up and turned me around…

I Can't Hold My Peace!

EXEGESIS - What do we mean when we say I can't hold my peace? I can't hold <u>see-o-pah-o</u> (Gk) <u>see-gay</u> - I can't be silent, calm, or tightlipped. I cannot maintain my hay-soo-khee-os. I can't be still. I can't be reserved. I can't be restrained.

I. In our text, we find that the leaders of the crowd, those who were out front did not want Bartimaeus to cry out unto the Lord. In our day, we too face the same obstacles that Bartimaeus did. Many of our leaders, the people in the front do not want us to call on the Lord and disturb them.

   1. Thirty years ago a petition was circulated nationwide to silence prayer in the public school systems. Children not only cannot pray together in school. They cannot collectively bless food at school. And we wonder what's wrong with our schools? Why so many shootings? Why so much violence? It's because God has been unceremoniously expelled from school.

   2. In your home, have you ever attempted to witness to that son or daughter, husband or wife about the goodness of Jesus Christ and values of a Christian life only to be met with "Get out of my face, I don't want to hear that? You ain't always been saved."

3. Have you ever approached a friend who was in obvious trouble and despair and attempted to share with them the word of God only to have them tell you to "Shut-up, get out of my face with that Christian stuff?"
4. You try to speak up for the Lord, but everywhere you turn someone is saying, "Be quiet. Hold your peace!"

II. Even in the church, the enemy wants us to hold our peace. The enemy wants us to stay still and stay quiet. The leaders of the crowd, the ones out front don't want any disruption from their parade. They want the praise, they want the glory, and they want the accolades.

1. When you say Amen, they look at you as if you were crazy. (Be quiet. We don't <u>say</u> that here.) But Psa. 41:13 says, "Blessed be the Lord God of Israel from everlasting and to everlasting. Amen and Amen."
2. When you clap your hands, they look at you as if you've lost your mind . (Be quiet. That's not considered <u>proper</u> here.) But Ps. 47:1 says, "O clap your hands, all ye people; shout unto God with the voice of triumph."

3. When you shout hallelujah, they look at you with shock! (Be quiet. That's not considered <u>dignified</u> here.) But Rev 19:1 says, "And after these things I heard a great voice and much people in heaven, saying, Alleluia; Salvation and glory and honor and power, unto the Lord our God".

4. When you dance a holy dance in the isles, they look at you with scorn. (Be still. That's not appropriate here.) But II Samuel 6:14 says. . . "David danced before the Lord with all his might; and David was girded with a linen ephod."

5. When you sing to the glory of God, they look at you with disdain. Be quiet. It doesn't take that much in here.) But Psa. 144:9 says, "I will sing a new song unto thee, O God: upon a psaltery and an instrument of 10 strings will I sing praises unto thee."

6. When you stand up and testify and give witness of the goodness of God, they analyze you . (Be quiet. We don't have time for all that.) But Psa. 107:2 says, "Let the redeemed of the Lord say so,

whom he hath redeemed from the hand of the enemy."

7. You must be careful of those out front. They don't want you to cause them any embarrassment. They want you to stay quiet… They want you to be politically correct. But don't you pay them any attention … Tell Satan to get behind you … Tell that demon, for God I live and for God I die.

8. You just call on our redeemer … Praise God in his sanctuary … Praise him for his mighty acts … Praise him with the sound of the trumpet … Praise him with the timbrel and dance … Praise him upon the loud cymbals … Let everything that has breath praise the Lord. (Psalms 150) David said, "I will bless the Lord at all times: his praise shall continually be in my mouth (Psa. 34:1)." I can't hold my peace!

   II. When you have the spirit of the Lord on the inside, something must happen on the outside… The prophet Ezekiel called it a, "Wheel in the middle of a wheel". Isaiah declared… "Ye that make mention of the Lord keep not silence".

1. <u>Jeremiah</u> confessed, "Then I said, I will not make mention of him, nor speak any more in his name. But his word was in mine heart as a burning fire shut up in my bones!"
2. Jesus told the Pharisees, who demanded that he hush the grateful crowd as he entered Jerusalem, "I tell you that if these should hold their peace, the stones would immediately cry out."
3. Jesus told Paul, "Be not afraid, but speak and hold not thy peace: For I am with thee, and no man set on thee to hurt thee"….
4. I can hear my ancestors singing at revival meeting, "Said I wasn't gonna tell nobody but I couldn't keep it to myself what the Lord has done for me. You oughta been there when he saved my soul. You oughta been there when he put my name on the roll…"

CONCLUSION - I want to encourage you to call on the name of Jesus anywhere, anytime. Don't let anyone, anywhere, anytime stand in your way. Don't let the devil and his flunkies steal your blessings. If you want joy, if you want peace, if you want salvation, if you want the inheritance of eternal life, if you want heaven's window to open in your life, remember when <u>praises</u> go up, then blessings come down. If you want it, God's got it; he's got everything I need: food, money, health, and strength. The earth is the Lord's. The beast in the fields and the cattle on a thousand hills. The silver and gold for my Father is rich in houses and land.

When I think of the goodness of Jesus Christ and all that he has done for me, my soul cries hallelujah, I thank God for saving me! I can't hold My Peace.

Someone will ask me, "Why can't you contain yourself". Because this is the day that the Lord has made, I will rejoice and be glad in it. I can't restrain myself, because the Lord I serve inhabits the praise of the saints. I'm happy because while I was yet a sinner, Christ died for me, yes even a wretch like me.

I've got to tell somebody that when he died I went from accused to acquitted … bewildered to blessed … condemned to converted … guilty to grace … heartbroken to healed … ignorant to informed … jacked-up to joy … knocked down to kneel down …

lost to loved ... messed up to made up, overwhelmed to overcomer ... puffed up to prayed up ... quantity to quality ... rejection to redemption ... stagnation to salvation ... transgressor to transformer ... undesirable to undeniable ... violated to vindicated ... wasteful to watchful ... excommunicated to exonerated ... yoked to yielded ... zero to hero!

~ June 29, 2007

The Expedient Route

"Nor consider that it is expedient for us, that one man should die for the people, and that the whole nation perish not" (John 11:50).

After Jesus raised Lazarus from the dead in the hill region of Bethany, many once skeptical Jews believed that he was the Son of God. Seemingly all of his miracles won him disciples and increased his fame, but raising a man from the grave after being dead four days was arguably his greatest miracle. So much so that those loyal to the established Jewish leadership rushed back to the Pharisees to alert them to what Jesus had done.

The chief priest called an emergency meeting of the 70 Sanhedrin council members. There was only one item on the agenda, "What shall we do about Jesus of Nazareth?" He was becoming an increasing threat to the status quo and their political and economic strangle hold on the nation.

After much debate, the high priest Caiaphas, though vile and degenerate in his heart, spoke into the atmosphere words of Messianic salvation. He said, "You do not understand that it is expedient for you that one man should die for the people, and that the whole nation should not perish." These cold words of conspiracy triggered the week of passion and ultimately our Savior's tragic death on Calvary.

In our attempts to control situations or manipulate people, we often choose the most expedient route. This route is often selected because it is self-gratifying. Close examination of the expedient route will reveal a road cluttered and crowed with the atrocities of man's inhumanity to his fellow man.

The Sanhedrin Council went to great lengths to manufacture Jesus' ultimate defeat, yet he warned them of what would happen to the world if they carried out their devious plot. He declared, "If I be lifted up from the earth, I will draw all men unto me". Killing Jesus gave his detractors momentary joy, but it gave his disciples a perpetual Savior.

Nineteen hundred years later, one of those drawn to that victim of expediency would lead an oppressed people out of a wilderness of disenfranchisement towards the Promised Land of social and economic equality. After assembling more than 250,000 people at the Lincoln Memorial in peaceful protest for jobs and freedom in 1963, after winning the Noble Peace Prize in 1964, after securing the Voting Rights Act of 1965, and speaking against the Vietnam War in 1967, the forces of evil wanted to know, "What shall we do about Martin Luther King, Jr.? If we don't stop him soon, his 'war on poverty' will disrupt the status quo and expose our capitalistic greed".

It was expedient to assassinate Dr. King in Memphis, Tennessee, the day after he declared, "I've been to the mountaintop and I've seen the Promised Land". Killing Dr. King gave his detractors temporary relief, but 15 years later, his supporters would celebrate his birthday as a national holiday. Kind of ironic is it not?

Joseph's commentary on these pivotal events in history is, "But as for you, you thought evil against me; but God meant it for good, to bring it to pass, as it is this day, to save much people alive" (Gen. 50:20).

On Easter Sunday, we remember Christ who got up from the dead and Martin King to whom Jesus promised, "I am the resurrection, and the life: he that believeth in me, though he were dead, yet shall he live" (John 11:25).

~ April 1, 2010

George Bernard Jackson is the youngest son of Dr. William T. and Pearlena M. Jackson of Salisbury, North Carolina. He was born on March 20, 1962 in Rock Hill, South Carolina. He is a 1980 graduate of Chester Senior High School in Chester, South Carolina. He attended North Carolina Central University in Durham, North Carolina graduating with a Bachelor of Arts degree in Political Science.

Jackson received the Master of Divinity degree with honors in May 1996 from Shaw Divinity, Raleigh, NC. He later received the Doctor of Ministry degree from Friends International Christian University, Merced, California in October 1998. Jackson also received the Doctor of Ministry in Pastoral Care, May 2009, Gardner-Webb University, Boiling Springs, NC.

Jackson is the founding Pastor/CEO of Citadel Ministries, Thomasville, North Carolina. He has been in ministry for 27 years and the pastoral ministry for 26 years. He is also founder and president of United Cornerstone School of Divinity, 2005. A community activist, Jackson is founder and chairman of the Martin Luther King Social Action Committee, Inc.

He has dedicated this labor of love to the edifying of God's people and building the cherished, "Beloved Community." Jackson is married to the lovely Pamela Ann Stanfield. They are the proud parents of six children and five grandchildren.

Bibliography

Allwood, Josiah K., *"Uncloudy Day"*, 1880

Caesar, Shirley, *"This Joy I Have"*, Artemis Gospel, 1999

DeVaughn, William, *"Be Thankful for What You Got"*, Omega Sound, 1972

Douglas, C. N., *"Forty Thousand Quotations"*, 1917

Gabriel, Charles H. and Martin, Civilla D., *"His Eye is On the Sparrow"*, 1905

Griffiths, Marcia, *"Electric Boogie"*, Mango/Island Records, 1989

Hiscox, Edward T., *"Hiscox Guide for Baptist Churches"*, 1964

King, Martin Luther Jr., *"Remaining Awake Through a Great Revolution"*, Oberlin College, 1965

Lowell, James Russell, *"The Present Crisis"*, 1914

Mote, Edward, *"Hymns of Praise"*, 1836

Stern, David H., *"Complete Jewish Bible"*, 1998

U.S. Business Cycle Expansions and Contractions, *Nation Bureau of Economic Research*, 2009

Wesley, Charles, *"A Collection of Psalms and Hymns"*, 1741

Wiesel, Elie, *"Nobel Prize Acceptance Speech"*, 1986

Wilcox, Ella Wheeler, *"Poems of Problems"*, 1914 pg. 154

Made in the USA
Charleston, SC
15 November 2015